CAMBRIDGE PRIMARY
English

Learner's Book

4

Sally Burt and Debbie Ridgard

CAMBRIDGE
UNIVERSITY PRESS

CAMBRIDGE
UNIVERSITY PRESS

University Printing House, Cambridge CB2 8BS, United Kingdom

Cambridge University Press is part of the University of Cambridge.

It furthers the University's mission by disseminating knowledge in the pursuit of education, learning and research at the highest international levels of excellence.

Information on this title: education.cambridge.org

© Cambridge University Press 2015

This publication is in copyright. Subject to statutory exception and to the provisions of relevant collective licensing agreements, no reproduction of any part may take place without the written permission of Cambridge University Press.

First published 2015
6th printing 2016

Printed in the United Kingdom by Latimer Trend

A catalogue record for this publication is available from the British Library

ISBN 978-1-107-67566-7 Paperback

Cambridge University Press has no responsibility for the persistence or accuracy of URLs for external or third-party internet websites referred to in this publication, and does not guarantee that any content on such websites is, or will remain, accurate or appropriate. Information regarding prices, travel timetables, and other factual information given in this work is correct at the time of first printing but the publishers do not guarantee the accuracy of such information thereafter.

....

NOTICE TO TEACHERS
It is illegal to reproduce any part of this work in material form (including photocopying and electronic storage) except under the following circumstances:
(i) where you are abiding by a licence granted to your school or institution by the Copyright Licensing Agency;
(ii) where no such licence exists, or where you wish to exceed the terms of a licence, and you have gained the written permission of Cambridge University Press;
(iii) where you are allowed to reproduce without permission under the provisions of Chapter 3 of the Copyright, Designs and Patents Act 1988, which covers, for example, the reproduction of short passages within certain types of educational anthology and reproduction for the purposes of setting examination questions.

Contents

	Introduction	5

1 Storybook 6

1	What makes a story a story?	6
2	Extend your reading range	8
3	Read and present an extract	9
4	Check your understanding	12
5	Work with verb tenses	12
6	Explore beginnings	15
7	Focus on character and setting	16
8	Creating mind pictures from detail	19
9	Find out more about the story	19
10	Practise using punctuation to read for meaning	21
11	Write a story starter competition entry	21
12	Write a story introduction	23

2 Going deep 24

1	Talk about the sea	24
2	Dictionary work	26
3	Identify root words	27
4	Ordering information	28
5	Words in context	30
6	Work with sentences	32
7	Revise and use sentences, phrases and key words	33
8	Summarise the main idea	34
9	Looking at tenses	38
10	Work with connectives	39
11 and 12	Collect information for an oral presentation	40

3 Mind pictures 41

1	Use your imagination	41
2	Meet a modern poet who uses kennings	44
3	Plan and write a kenning poem	47
4	What is a colour?	49
5	Focus on poetic technique	51
6	Write a colour poem	53

4 Just imagine 54

1	Read a blurb	54
2	*Harry's Mad*	56
3	Understand the plot	57
4	Read more about Harry and Mad	59
5	Present a dramatic reading	60
6	Check your understanding	62
7	Work with adverbs	62
8	Learn more about apostrophes	63
9	*The Voyages of Doctor Dolittle*	64
10	Focus on language	66
11	Make notes for a storyboard	67
12	Present a storyboard of *The Lion and the Mouse*	69

5 Making the news 70

1	Share information	70
2	Link it up	71
3	Research information	73
4	Building words	75
5	Compare information texts	77
6	Ask questions	78

7	Ordering information	80
8	Write a headline	81
9	Use varying tenses	82
10	Keeping things in order	83
11 and 12	Write a news article	85

6 Sensational poems 86
1	Talk about it	86
2	Hear the sounds	87
3	Rhyming patterns	89
4	Assonance	90
5	Punctuation gives expression	91
6	Shape poems	92

7 What would you do? 94
1	Food for thought	94
2	Making difficult decisions	97
3	Summarise your understanding	99
4	Focus on the language	100
5	Work with sentences	101
6	What would you do?	102
7	Notice the language	104
8	Degrees of comparison	105
9	*Cool!*	107
10	Read about Robbie's classmates	109
11	Explore how play scripts work	111
12	Perform a play script	113

8 Food for thought 114
1	Introducing persuasive language	114
2	Be descriptive	116
3	Compare layout, purpose, language	117
4	Analyse an advertisement	119
5	Design an advertisement	121
6	Introduce yourself	121
7	Write a personal profile	122
8	A promotional review	123
9	Adverbs of degree	125
10	Be persuasive	126
11 and 12	Present a persuasive speech	127

9 Poems to ponder 130
1	Poems that play with words	130
2	Discuss poetic technique	132
3	Prepare and perform a poem	133
4	Moon poem	135
5	Appreciate the poem	137
6	Write a sun poem	139

Spelling activities 140

Term 1 – Root words; Compound words; Syllables; Letter patterns and sounds; Silent letters; Word endings

Term 2 – Adding suffixes; -logy word families; Build word families; Vowel sounds; Homophones can trip you up!

Term 3 – Comparative spelling; Root words; Nifty numbers; Cardinal and ordinal numbers; Short and long vowel sounds

Toolkit 146

Parts of speech and articles; Punctuation; Reading skills; Poet's corner; Looking for information; The writing process; Reading aloud essentials; Exercise your listening skills; Editor's handbook

Acknowledgements 154

Welcome to the *Cambridge Primary English* Series, Stage 4.

This Learner's Book will take you through Stage 4 of the Cambridge Primary curriculum. It contains nine units of lessons and activities to develop your reading, writing, speaking and listening skills. This book covers all the skills you need to develop in Stage 4!

Three units focus on fiction, three on non-fiction and three on poetry and plays. Each unit has a theme covering a variety of topics so that there's something for everyone. You'll enjoy texts and extracts from a range of stories, legends, fables, accounts, recounts, biographies, autobiographies, diaries, journals and different types of poems. They have been carefully selected to reflect as many different interests as possible. The texts will teach you about language and allow you to communicate and express yourself in different ways.

Sometimes, your teacher will lead a discussion or explain the activity; sometimes you'll work in small groups or with a talk partner; at other times, you'll work alone. Some activities need you to listen for specific information while other activities ask you to read aloud or perform a role play.

These icons will show you how you're going to work:

- have a discussion
- do some reading
- do some writing
- role play, read out loud or do an oral activity
- AZ do a spelling activity

The activities are designed to develop your reading, writing, listening and speaking skills and to explore, investigate, understand, use and develop your knowledge of English.

Here are some things to look out for:

Hello! I am here to guide and help you.

Tip
These tips give you handy hints as you work.

Did you know?
These boxes provide interesting information and opportunities for further research.

How did I do?
These boxes help you check your own progress along the way.

Language focus
These boxes will explain specific language rules.

On pages 140 to 145 you'll find interesting and enjoyable spelling rules and activities to practise and expand your knowledge of spelling. You can go there whenever you like to check your own spelling skills or to learn more about common spelling patterns and letter strings.

On pages 146 to 153 you'll find a Toolkit – a set of resources for you to use at any time. These include tools and tips such as an editing checklist, a self-evaluation tool for reading aloud and a list of group work rules.

We hope you enjoy the course and that it helps you feel confident about responding to English, and using English in a variety of ways.

Sally Burt and Debbie Ridgard

1 Storybook

Stories come in all shapes and sizes – long, short, funny and sad. In this unit, you'll discuss the stories you enjoy and decide for yourself what makes a good story. You'll develop your skills at choosing books to read, and write an exciting story introduction!

Vocabulary to learn and use:
story, author, fiction, genre, character, plot, setting, introduction, conclusion, resolution, extract, tale

1 What makes a story a story?

A **AZ** Revise your understanding of 'story talk' by matching each definition below to a word in the vocabulary box.

- The writer of a story, play or poem
  author
- A person, animal or fictional being in a story
- The ending of a story
- A passage taken from a story
- A synonym for 'story'
- Stories about events that have not really happened
- The beginning of a story
- The storyline, or sequence of events that makes up a story, play or novel
- The solving of a problem
- The place or places where a story takes place
- A real or imaginary account of an event or series of events, for others to see, hear, read or feel
- The type of story

B In a group, discuss some of the first stories you remember hearing. Stories have existed for thousands of years – ever since people could talk. Some stories are written down but others are remembered and told for generations, changing along the way as each teller adds a little to the tale.

Did you know?

Tale, yarn, legend, myth, fable, anecdote, account, narrative and chronicle are all **synonyms** for stories.

synonym *n.* a word or phrase that means the same, or almost the same, as another word or phrase

1. What sort of stories were they?
2. Were they fact, fiction, or a mix of both?
3. Who told you the stories?
4. Did you hear them once or more than once?
5. Which story did you enjoy most? Why?

Did you know?

Have you ever felt a braille storybook? Braille is a written language for the blind. Patterns of raised dots make words and are felt and read with the fingertips.

Take turns with a talk partner to retell a favourite story. Describe the setting and main characters.
1. Explain what genre it is.
2. Summarise the main events. 'Summarise' means don't give too much detail.
3. Explain why you enjoy your story.
4. Comment on whether you've heard each other's story before, or a different version of it.

Any volunteers? Who'd like to retell their favourite story to the class?

Session 1 What makes a story a story?

7

2 Extend your reading range

A 🗨 **Discuss with a talk partner what you like in a story.**

1 Use the features below to help your discussion.

Characters similar to me or my age	Unusual, quirky characters
Animals that talk or act like people	Imaginary or faraway places
An adventure or exciting events	Humour
Traditional or familiar characters	Real life issues
Unexpected or unlikely events	Happy endings
	Sad or unclear endings

2 Look at your independent readers and discuss their features.

3 Write two or three sentences in your notebook explaining what you enjoy in a story. Begin like this: *I enjoy ... because ...*

4 Exchange sentences with your partner to check for:
- sentences that start with capital letters and end with full stops
- at least one verb in each sentence
- correct spelling.

Tip

Knowing what you like in a story helps you choose books you'll enjoy.

B 📖 🗨 **Choose a book for each other from the school or class library. Try to choose something you think your partner wouldn't normally read.**

1 Review any information on the cover of the book chosen for you.
2 Read the beginning of the book.
3 Tell your partner whether you think you'd enjoy it. Give reasons using the words **genre**, **character** and **setting**.

Why not read the rest of the book? I challenge you to try something new!

8 Unit 1 Storybook

C 📝 **AZ** Start a reading log to record all your reading, including non-fiction.

1 Fill in details about your independent reader and comment on what you did or didn't enjoy. Use appropriate presentation writing.

Tip

Keeping a record of everything you read helps you remember what you did and didn't enjoy.

Date	Title	Author	Genre	Comment
6th September	The Legend of Spud Murphy	Eoin Colfer		

spud n. potato (informal)

3 Read and present an extract

A 👥 In groups of four, prepare to read aloud an extract from *The Legend of Spud Murphy*. Discuss these questions about the book's title.

1 Do you think 'Spud' is a real name? Give reasons.
2 What does it mean if someone is described as a 'legend'?
3 Make a list of people you think are modern day legends.
4 What and whom do you think the book will be about? Will it be humorous or serious?

B 📖💬 Stories are often told in narrative and dialogue. You can improve your expression while reading if you can tell the difference.

1 Skim the extract to find out who narrates the story. How can you tell?
2 Scan it to establish how many people speak in the extract.

Did you know?

Speech marks show when a character starts and stops talking. Question marks and exclamation marks show the expression.

Language focus

Narrative is when the narrator tells the story.
Dialogue is the words characters say to each other, enclosed by speech marks.
   "Don't make us join the library," Marty begged. *"It's too dangerous."*
A new line is started whenever a different person speaks.

Session 3 Read and present an extract

The Legend of Spud Murphy

Marty tried to save us. "Remember the last educational hobby? The art classes? I was
⁵ sick for days."

"That was your own fault," said Mum.

"I only had a drink of water."

"You are not supposed to drink
¹⁰ the water that people use to wash their brushes."

Dad was thinking. "What about the library?" he said finally.

"What about it?" I said, trying to sound casual, but my
¹⁵ stomach was churning.

"You both could join. Reading. It's perfect. How can you cause trouble reading a book?"

"And it's educational," added Mum.

"Yes, of course, it's educational too," Dad agreed.

²⁰ "How is it educational?" I asked, terrified by the idea.
"I'd much rather be outside riding a horse than inside reading about one."

My mother tousled my hair. "Because, Will, sometimes the only horse you can ride is the one in your head."
²⁵ I had no idea what that meant.

"Don't make us join the library," Marty begged. "It's too dangerous."

"Dangerous? How could a library be dangerous?" Dad asked.

"It's not the library," Marty whispered. "It's the librarian."
³⁰ "Mrs Murphy?" said Mum. "She's a lovely old lady."

The problem with grown-ups is that they only see what's on the outside. But kids know the real truth. People forget to be on their best behaviour around kids, because nobody believes a word we say. Every kid in our town knew about
35 Mrs Murphy. She was one of those people that kids steer clear of.

"She's not a lovely old lady," I said. "She's a total nut."

"Will! That's a terrible thing to say."

"But she is, Mum. She hates kids and she used to be a
40 tracker in the army. Tracking kids from enemy countries."

"Now you're being ridiculous."

"She has a spud gun under her desk," added Marty. "A gas-powered one that takes an entire potato in the barrel. She shoots kids with it if they make a noise in the library.
45 That's why we call her Spud Murphy."

My mother thought this was all very funny. "A spud gun! You'll say anything to avoid reading a book."

Eoin Colfer

Prepare to read the extract aloud and present your performance.
1 Decide who will take each role (Narrator (Will), Mum, Dad, Marty).
2 Discuss how to make your reading interesting to listen to.
   How will each person speak? Try out some ideas and practise your reading together.
   - Use the punctuation to know when to pause or add expression.
   - Use body language as well as expression.
3 Present your reading aloud for another group.

Why do you think reading silently is faster than reading aloud?

Session 3 Read and present an extract　**11**

4 Check your understanding

A 📖 📝 Use close reading to answer these questions in your notebook.
1. What does Mum want the boys to do?
2. What happened to the family's last educational hobby?
3. Why is Will's stomach churning?
4. Who is Spud Murphy?
5. Summarise Mum's and Will's descriptions of Spud Murphy. Which is more likely to be accurate?
6. How would you react if you were told to join your library?

How did I do?

- Did I answer all the questions?
- Did I use evidence from the text in my answers?
- Did I express my ideas clearly?
- Did I write my answers as full sentences?

B 📝 Complete your reading log for the extract from *The Legend of Spud Murphy*. Write a comment about whether you would enjoy reading the rest of the book.

5 Work with verb tenses

Language focus

Verbs tell you what someone or something **does**, **is**, or **has**. Verb **tenses** are different forms of the verb that show **when** it takes place: whether it has already happened, is happening now or will happen in the future.

He drank a glass of water earlier. (past tense)

She drinks a glass of water every morning. (present tense)

They will drink a glass of water later. (future tense)

Unit 1 Storybook

A Stories are usually in the past tense because they describe events that have already taken place. It's important to keep the tense consistent so the reader doesn't get confused.

1 **Say each sentence aloud using the correct tense of the verb to tell to help you.**
   a Marty tries to save us and (*tell*) Mum about the last educational hobby.
   b Marty tried to save us and (*tell*) Mum about the last educational hobby.

2 **Replace *tell* in each sentence with the correct tense of the verbs *remind*, *inform* and *alert*.**

How do the different verbs change the effect of the sentence?

B Change regular verbs into the past tense by adding the suffix **ed** to the root word.

You look at the book. You looked at the book.

1 **Write the paragraph below in the past tense in your notebook, choosing suitable verbs from the box.**

| visualise | glare | sigh | close | change | churn |

Will's stomach (*verb*) as he (*verb*) Mrs Murphy in his mind. Her image (*verb*) at him, spud gun at the ready. He (*verb*) his eyes and (*verb*) deeply. Mum never (*verb*) her mind.

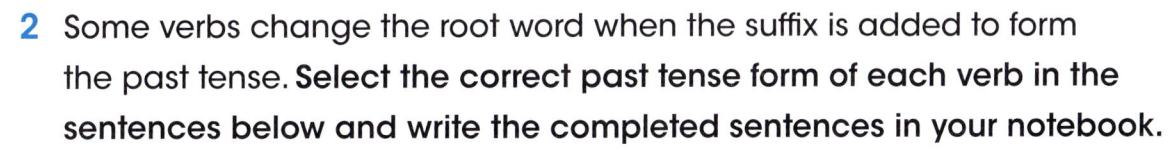

2 Some verbs change the root word when the suffix is added to form the past tense. **Select the correct past tense form of each verb in the sentences below and write the completed sentences in your notebook.**
   a Will (*love*) reading so when he (*arrive*) at the library, he (*hope*) Spud Murphy had (*decide*) to take the day off.
   b Will (*try*) to explain that all the children were (*worry*) about Spud Murphy. Once she (*spy*) you, you were in trouble!

Tip

If the verb ends in **e**, just add **d**.

If the verb ends in **y**, the **y** changes to **i** before adding **ed**.

Verbs that don't follow a rule for forming the past tense are called **irregular** verbs.

Session 5 Work with verb tenses

3 Match each present tense verb to its irregular past tense partner.

Present tense	Past tense
read	thought
say	read
think	was
find	found
is	had
have	said

4 Use three of these verbs in sentences of your own, as if you were adding to the extract.

C With a talk partner, explore the verb tenses in the *Spud Murphy* extract.
1 Read some of the dialogue to each other. Is it in the present or past tense? How can you tell?
2 What tense is the narrative text?
3 What does this tell you about using verb tenses in stories?

Any volunteers? Who'd like to share their ideas with the class?

D Some verbs such as *said, asked* and *replied* are used so often they become boring. Use descriptive or expressive verbs to make a story more engaging to read.
1 Investigate the effect of different verbs. In a small group read the sentence in the box below aloud and try out different verbs in place of *begged*.
2 Discuss how different verbs change the effect of what Marty says.
3 Which of the verbs fit Marty's and Will's mood in the extract?

Did you know?
Verbs that tell us how the person is feeling when they speak create an effect called **mood**.

said   gasped   cried   whispered   sobbed   pleaded
laughed   wailed   implored   muttered   chuckled

"Don't make us join the library," Marty begged.

14 Unit 1 Storybook

6 Explore beginnings

A 💬 The beginning of a story should grab your attention. It should provide enough information about the plot, characters or setting to get you hooked and make you want to read on.

Discuss in a small group.
1 Re-read the first sentence of the *Spud Murphy* extract and discuss how it grabs attention.
2 Predict the main characters and the main setting.
3 Decide if Spud Murphy will be more like the description given by Marty or his mother.
4 Explain whether the extract makes you want to read the rest of the story.
5 Summarise your group's ideas in a few sentences to share with the class.

B 📝 Create a story map similar to the one below. Write key words to describe what you discovered about the main characters, setting and plot.

Tip
Your key words can be nouns, adjectives, verbs or adverbs. Choose interesting key words that really remind you of the story details.

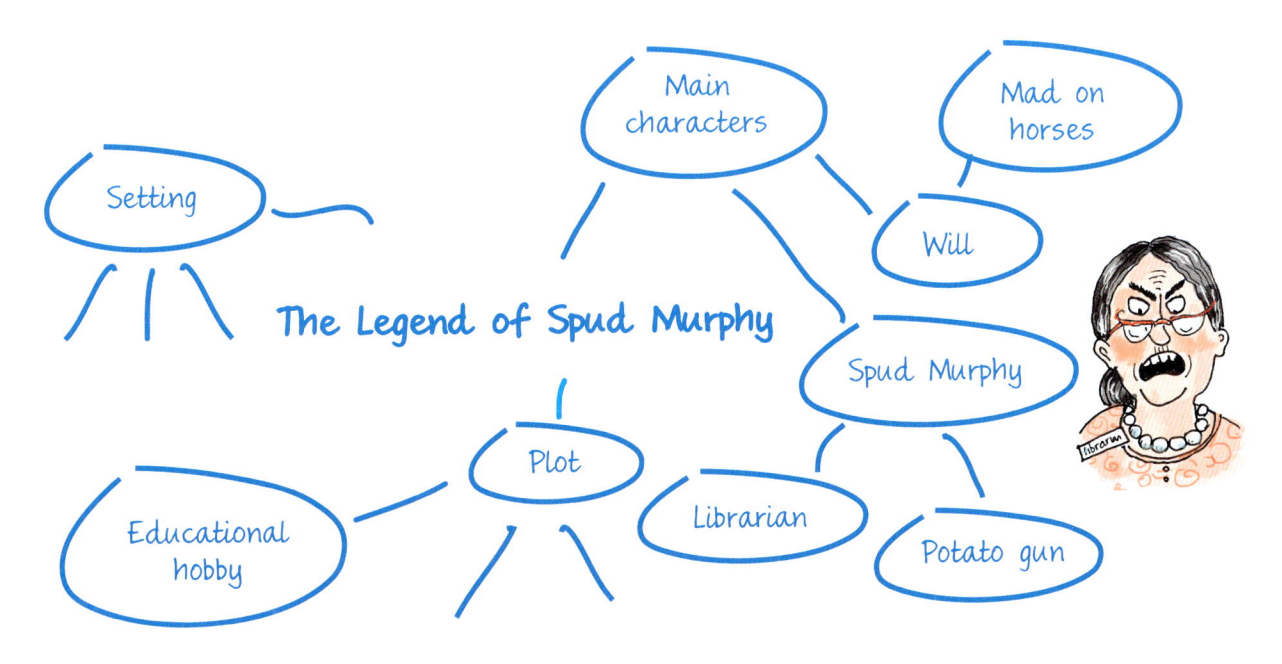

Story map: The Legend of Spud Murphy
- Setting
- Main characters
  - Will — Mad on horses
  - Spud Murphy — Librarian, Potato gun
- Plot
  - Educational hobby

Session 6 Explore beginnings 15

7 Focus on character and setting

A Read the extract from a fantasy story. With a talk partner, scan for some details.

1 Who is the main character?
2 What is the setting?

Where the Mountain Meets the Moon

Chapter 1

Far away from here, following the Jade River, there was once a black mountain that <u>cut into</u> the sky like a jagged piece of rough metal. The villagers called it Fruitless Mountain because nothing grew on it and birds and animals did not rest there.

Crowded in the corner of where Fruitless Mountain and the Jade River met was a village that was a shade of faded brown. This was because the land around the village was hard and poor. To <u>coax</u> rice out of the stubborn land, the fields had to be flooded with water. The villagers had to <u>tramp</u> in the mud, bending and stooping and planting day after day. Working in the mud so much made it spread everywhere and the hot sun dried it onto their clothes and hair and homes. Over time, everything in the village had become the dull color of dried mud. → 1

One of the houses in this village was so small that its wood boards, held together by the roof, made one think of a bunch of matches tied with a piece of twine. Inside, there was barely enough room for three people to sit around the table – which was lucky because only three people lived there. One of them was a young girl called Minli.

Minli was not brown and dull like the rest of the village. She had glossy black hair with pink cheeks, shining eyes always eager for adventure, and a fast smile that <u>flashed</u> from her face. When people saw her lively and impulsive spirit, they thought her name, which meant *quick thinking*, suited her well. "Too well," her mother sighed, as Minli had a habit of quick acting as well. → 2

Ma sighed a great deal, an impatient noise usually accompanied with a frown at their rough clothes, rundown house, or meager food. Minli could not remember a time when Ma did not sigh; it often made Minli wish she had been called a name that meant *gold* or *fortune* instead. Because Minli and her parents, like the village and the land around them, were very poor. They were barely able to harvest enough rice to feed themselves, and the only money in the house was two old copper coins that sat in a blue rice bowl with a white rabbit painted on it. The coins and the bowl belonged to Minli; they had been given to her when she was a baby, and she had had them for as long as she could remember.

What kept Minli from becoming dull and brown like the rest of the village were the stories her father told her every night at dinner. She <u>glowed</u> with such wonder and excitement that even Ma would smile, though she would shake her head at the same time. Ba seemed to drop his gray and work weariness – his black eyes <u>sparkled</u> like raindrops in the sun when he began a story.

"Ba, tell me the story about Fruitless Mountain again," Minli would say as her mother spooned their plain rice into bowls. "Tell me again why nothing grows on it."

"Ah," Minli's father said, "you've heard this so many times. You know."

"Tell me again, Ba," Minli begged. "Please."

"Okay," he said, and as he set down his chopsticks his smile twinkled in a way that Minli loved.

Grace Lin

Key to paragraphs:
1 setting
2 main character
3 character and plot details
4 more character details

color *n.* American spelling of *colour*
gray *n. a.* American spelling of *grey*
meager *a.* American spelling of *meagre*; (of amounts) very small or not enough

Session 7 Focus on character and setting

B 📖 💬 Paragraphs organise the ideas in a text. Writers start a new paragraph for a different action, time, place, thought or speaker.

Tip
The first words in a paragraph often contain a clue to the main idea.

1 Order the main ideas of the paragraphs in the extract.
   - Minli's home and family are introduced.
   - Minli asks her father to tell her a story (more than one paragraph).
   - The setting for the village is described.
   - Fruitless Mountain is introduced.
   - Why Minli is different is explained.
   - Clues about the plot are given.
2 Discuss why the author started each new paragraph.

C 📖 📝 Explore powerful, descriptive verbs.

1 Scan the extract for the underlined verbs. List them in alphabetical order.
2 Try to work out the meaning of each verb by reading it **in context**.
3 Match each word in your list to the word closest in meaning from the box below.

Reading a word **in context** means reading the words and sentences around it. It can help you understand new words without using a dictionary. You can still use your dictionary to check afterwards!

> caught the light   sharply outlined against   walk heavily
> had a warm healthy appearance   persuade   came readily

4 Use a thesaurus to find other descriptive verbs that could be used. Add them to your words to build mini word banks.
5 Choose one new verb to replace each of the underlined verbs in the extract. Make sure it fits the context.
6 With a talk partner, read the extract using your new verbs. What is the effect?

Did you know?
Thesaurus comes from the ancient Greek and Latin words meaning 'treasure' – a treasure chest of words to choose from to make your writing more descriptive and precise.

18 Unit 1 Storybook

8 Creating mind pictures from detail

A Re-read the extract with a talk partner.

1 Make two lists, noting down key words and phrases from the extract that tell you:

Setting
- the village's location
- its 'colour'
- the climate
- the villagers' problem

Character
- what Minli's name means
- how she's different from other villagers
- what makes her different.

2 What name would you give to Minli's village? Give reasons.
3 Discuss how the setting is similar to or different from the area where you live.
4 Draw your impression of the village and write two or three sentences explaining whether you would like to live there and why.

9 Find out more about the story

A Explore how book covers provide visual clues about a story.

1 In pairs, study three possible covers for *Where the Mountain Meets the Moon*.
   a Describe what you see on each cover.
   b What do the covers tell you about Minli and her surroundings?
   c Think of some descriptive nouns and adjectives to match each cover.
2 Which cover best fits your impression of the story so far?

Which one would make you want to read the story?

Session 9 Find out more about the story

B Find out more about a story by reading a book description.

1 What new information does the book description give you about the plot? Make a list of new information. Use key words only.

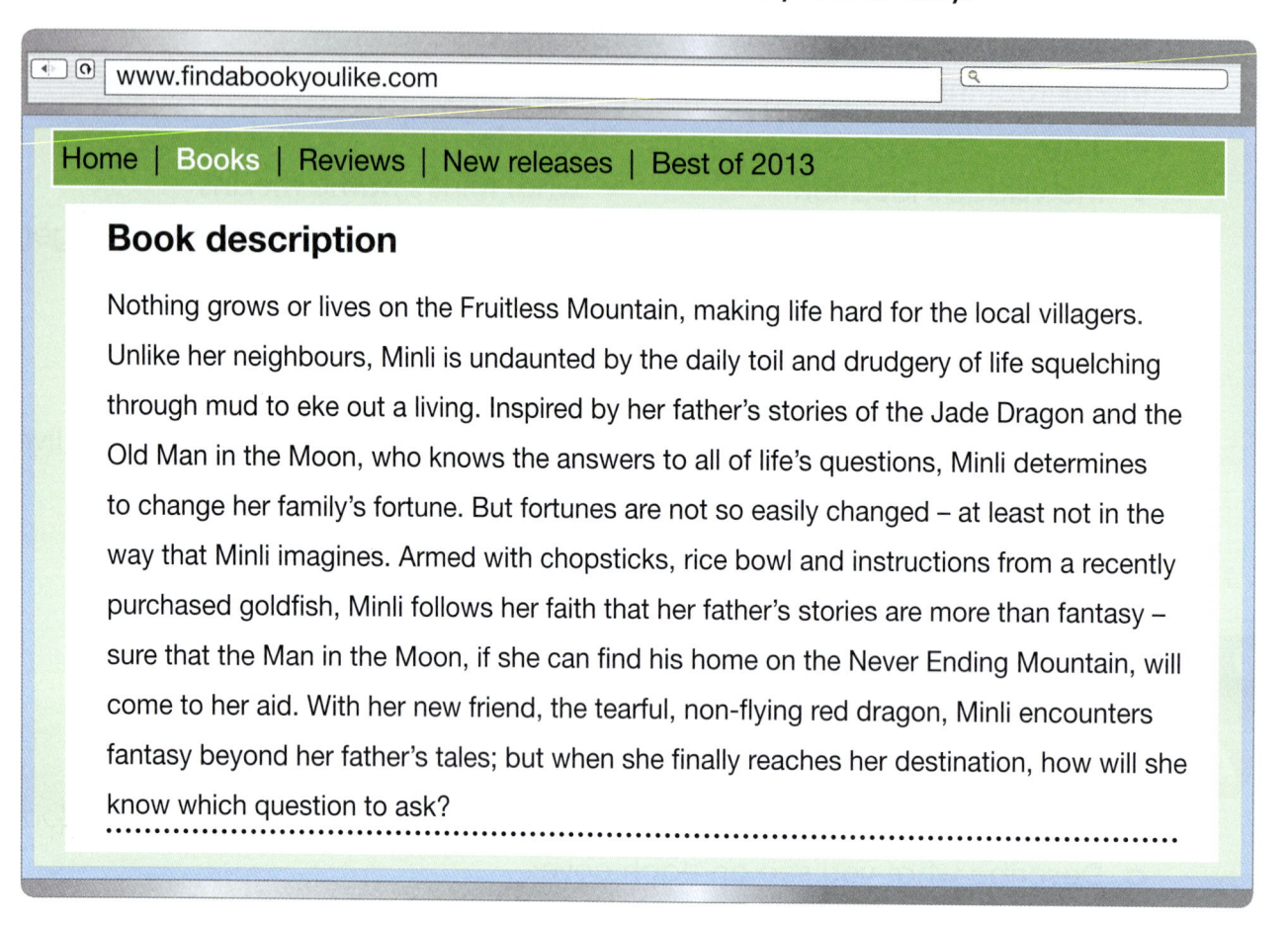

---

www.findabookyoulike.com

Home | Books | Reviews | New releases | Best of 2013

Book description

Nothing grows or lives on the Fruitless Mountain, making life hard for the local villagers. Unlike her neighbours, Minli is undaunted by the daily toil and drudgery of life squelching through mud to eke out a living. Inspired by her father's stories of the Jade Dragon and the Old Man in the Moon, who knows the answers to all of life's questions, Minli determines to change her family's fortune. But fortunes are not so easily changed – at least not in the way that Minli imagines. Armed with chopsticks, rice bowl and instructions from a recently purchased goldfish, Minli follows her faith that her father's stories are more than fantasy – sure that the Man in the Moon, if she can find his home on the Never Ending Mountain, will come to her aid. With her new friend, the tearful, non-flying red dragon, Minli encounters fantasy beyond her father's tales; but when she finally reaches her destination, how will she know which question to ask?

C In your notebook, jot down answers to the following questions.

1 Which words in the title tell you that *Where the Mountain Meets the Moon* is a fantasy story?
2 What details in the book description also show it is fantasy?
3 Which of these plots might be the story's main idea? Be ready to explain your ideas to the class.
   • Saving the village by finding a way to make things grow on Fruitless Mountain again.
   • Getting lost in a fantasy world on the moon.

D Complete your reading log for *Where the Mountain meets the Moon*. Say whether you would enjoy reading the rest of the story.

Unit 1 Storybook

10 Practise using punctuation to read for meaning

A Read the four sentences a–d below aloud with a talk partner.
1. Discuss the differences in meaning.
   a. Don't stop!
   b. Don't, stop!
   c. I like cooking my friends and chocolate.
   d. I like cooking, my friends and chocolate.

Tip
Commas show you where to pause when you read. They help you understand sentences properly.

2. The punctuation has gone missing from this paragraph! Can you make sense of it as you read it aloud?

minli loves her father's tales she is fascinated by the way his eyes light up and his body seems straighter and younger she never tires of hearing about the man in the moon the never ending mountain the bad tiger magistrate and places like the dragons gate or the village of the moon rain but most of all minli longs for home

B Practise reading the book description aloud.
- Read the book description in your head first, then softly out loud.
- Take note of the punctuation to make the meaning clear.

Any volunteers?
Who'd like to read the book description aloud, showing they can read the punctuation as well as the words?

1. With a talk partner, read out one paragraph each and give each other feedback.
   - Did you both manage all the pauses correctly?
   - Could you follow it easily? Did it make sense?
2. Practise reading the extract from *Where the Mountain Meets the Moon* to yourself, paying particular attention to the commas and other punctuation.

11 Write a story starter competition entry

A Read these fantasy story starters in a group.
1. Add a sentence to continue one of these story starters.
   a. Jed stepped cautiously through the doorway in the middle of the field.
   b. "Everybody, take cover!" barked the tree in the corner of the playground.

c "Where am I?" panicked Fatima, gaping at the unfamiliar room, filled with teeny-tiny furniture.

2 As a group, come up with another attention-grabbing story starter.

3 Exchange your new story starter with another group and continue each other's story starters sentence by sentence in your group.

4 Rate the story starters on this scale of how 'page-turning' they are.

deadly   boring   dull   ordinary   interesting   absorbing   intriguing   gripping   enthralling

B Enter the competition.

1 Design and fill in an entry form for the story starter competition. It is for Fantasy Fiction Publishers so your ideas should include something unlikely in real life. Follow the *Advice to entrants* to help you.

2 Come up with a list of ideas first and then try them out on a talk partner.

3 Finish your design and fill in your entry form.

Fantasy Story Starter Competition

Calling all writers! We need you!

How to enter: design your own entry form, including all the sections below to plan a fantasy story starter.

Uncover your talent and write a story starter for Fantasy Fiction Publishers.

Fame and Fortune Await!

Main character:
Setting:
Mood:
First sentence:

Fill in your entry form using key words and phrases.

Fantasy Fiction PUBLISHERS

Advice to entrants

People write well about what they know.

1 Choose somewhere you know for the setting and then add some unusual detail.

2 Think of a real person or a character you know well. Describe them and then change something about them – add a characteristic, change their age or family background.

3 Write a ripper of a first sentence! Make sure it contains something <u>impossible or unlikely to be true</u>. Be as fantastically creative as you can!

22 Unit 1 Storybook

12 Write a story introduction

A Fantasy Fiction Publishers liked the sound of your idea and want to see a draft with more detail.

How are all these words linked? Can you think of any others? fantasy, fantastic, fanciful, fantasise, fantasist, Fantasia, fancily

From: Fantasy Fiction Publishers
To: Entrant
Subject: Fantasy Story Starter Competition

Hi Fantastic Entrant,
We really enjoyed your fanciful story starter! Please send us three or four more paragraphs.
a Write it in the past tense (unless you are writing dialogue).
b Keep us captivated!
The Fantasy Fiction Publishers

Tip
Use the entry form to help add more detail to your sensational story starter.

1 In your notebook, jot down three to four paragraphs as an introduction to your story.

Tip
You won't have to write the rest of the story, so write whatever you like in the introduction! Why not use a mind map for your notes?

2 Swap your notes with a talk partner.
3 Give each other feedback on your ideas.
   a Does something unusual or unexpected happen?
   b Do you want to know what happens next?
4 Give each other ideas on how to improve your introduction.
5 Revise your draft with the new ideas.
6 Think of a creative way to illustrate and present your introduction to make it stand out to the publisher.

B Celebrate your success.
1 Practise presenting your introduction for the festival.
2 Enjoy listening to each other's introductions.
3 Have fun telling each other what you think could happen next after each introduction.

You've all been invited to the Fantasy Fiction story-telling festival.

2 Going deep

The sea is a great topic to explore if you like finding out about fascinating forms of life and amazing facts. In this unit you'll learn how to find the information you want from different types of texts. You'll practise organising your information so it makes sense and looks good, and you'll use your knowledge and skills to complete a project about your favourite sea creature.

Vocabulary to learn and use:
jellyfish, shellfish, fishing-rod, fisherman, seagoing, seafood, seaman, seahorse, octopus, tentacles, starfish, unique, barnacles

1 Talk about the sea

A What comes to mind when you think of 'the sea'? Have a discussion.

1 Take turns to say what you think the sea is like.
   Use your own words.
   Listen to how others describe the sea. Do you agree with them?
2 Share interesting facts that you know about the sea.
3 Here are some 'fishy facts' to add to your 'sea of knowledge'.
   Discuss how these facts are presented in an interesting way.
   Do the headings get your attention? How?

The 'sea of knowledge' is not a real sea. It's a figurative expression!

Flying fish?
Flying fish can leap out of the water and glide through the air using large fins like wings.

Best daddy?
The female seahorse lays her eggs in the male's pouch. He carries the eggs until they hatch – giving birth to the babies!

Who needs a dentist?
The ragged-tooth shark loses and replaces thousands of teeth in a lifetime.

Jellyfish for dessert?
The floating jelly-like body is harmless but watch out for the stinging tentacles below! Some jellyfish are lethal!

B Design your own Collector's Cards. Make up your own questions and fishy facts.

1 List some questions that you could use as interesting headings.

Do fish go to school?

Are there stars in the sea?

Is a seal a fish?

2 Discuss your questions to find out if anyone has any answers. Make notes.

Tip
Do some independent research to find out the answers to your questions.

C Riddles are an ancient form of entertainment. Listen to some and discuss possible solutions.

Alive without breath,
As cold as death;
Never thirsty, ever drinking,
All in mail, never clinking.

The Moon is my father,
The Sea is my mother;
I have a million brothers,
I die when I reach land.

Any volunteers?
Who can guess the answers? They are hidden on the next page.

Session 1 Talk about the sea 25

2 Dictionary work

A 🗨 **AZ** Identify the features of a dictionary.

Where do you begin to look for information? A dictionary is a good place to start.

1 Work with your talk partner; take turns to explain how a dictionary is organised.
2 Some words have more than one meaning. Which definitions will help you add information to your Collector's Cards?

Did you know?

Books are mostly categorised in two main groups:

Fiction: writing that is about unreal people, places, animals or events.

Non-fiction: writing that is factual and informative.

A **school** 1. *n.* a place where education is given 2. *n.* a group of people 3. *n.* a part of a university 4. *n.* a shoal of fish

B **seal** 1. *n.* a device for stamping a wax design 2. *n.* a sign of approval 3. *v.* to close something up 4. *v.* to settle the fate of something 5. *n.* an amphibious mammal

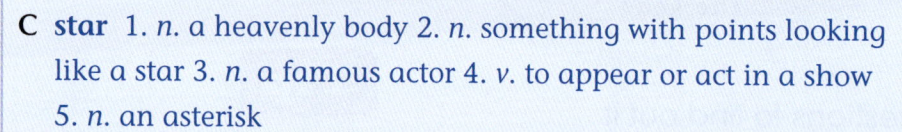

C **star** 1. *n.* a heavenly body 2. *n.* something with points looking like a star 3. *n.* a famous actor 4. *v.* to appear or act in a show 5. *n.* an asterisk

D **mail** 1. *n.* letters and parcels sent in the post 2. *v.* to send a letter by post 3. *n.* protective armour made from interlocking pieces or shell or scales of an animal

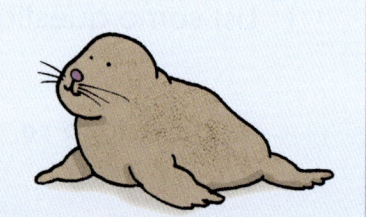

Riddle answers: fish, waves

abcdefghijklmno
pqrstuvwxyz

26 Unit 2 Going deep

B **AZ** Practise alphabetical order.

1 Rewrite these lists of words in alphabetical order:
   a ship, tanker, liner, hovercraft, ferry, canoe, boat, motorboat
   b rope, compass, deck, flag, mast, ore, rudder, anchor
   c pilchard, herring, trout, swordfish, hake, eel, sardine, sole

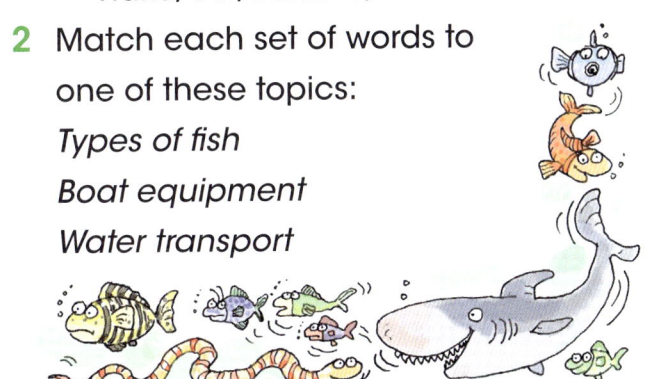

2 Match each set of words to one of these topics:
   Types of fish
   Boat equipment
   Water transport

> **Language focus**
>
> When you put words that begin with the same letter or letters into alphabetical order, you need to look at the next letter to know the order.
>
> seal   seam   seat
>
> These words have the same first three letters so you need to look at the fourth letter to know the correct order. **L** comes before **M**, and **M** comes before **T**.

How did I do?

- Can I say the alphabet from A to Z?
- Can I arrange words into alphabetical order?
- Can I use a dictionary to look up words and definitions?

3 Identify root words

A **AZ** A dictionary lists words and their meanings. Some words have similar meanings because they have the same **root words**.

A root word is a basic form of a word that may be added to, to make other words:

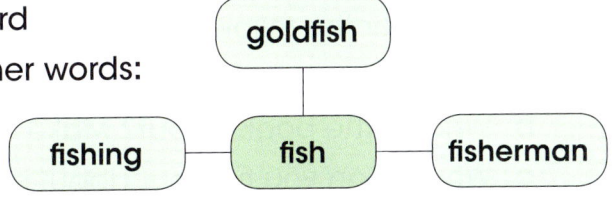

goldfish — fishing — fish — fisherman

1 Use a spider diagram to show the root word of group **a**, and group **b**.
   a seafood   undersea   seaman   overseas
   b fishing   jellyfish   fishing-rod   starfish

2 How many other examples of root words can you think of?

Session 3 Identify root words   **27**

B 🗨 **AZ**   Not all words with the same letters are connected. Some may look like they have the same root word but they have no link in meaning.

1   In the following lists, identify the common root word that connects *most* of the words.
    a   sailing, sailor, saint, sailplane
    b   shellfish, shelf, shells, shelling
    c   starlight, starry, stardust, start
    d   quicksand, sandal, sandy, sandbank
2   Which is the 'odd one out'? In each list identify the word that is not linked to the others. Use a dictionary to find the meaning.

4 Ordering information

A reference book provides information on a topic. The contents page and index have lists that tell you what is in a book and where to find it.

A 📖 🗨   Look at the layout of some magazines and information books.

1   With your talk partner discuss each layout.
    a   Does it have a contents page or an index or both?
    b   Where in the book are they positioned?
    c   What information does each page provide? Why is it useful?
    d   Identify similarities and differences between a contents page and an index.
    e   How are the other pages organised?
    f   Do these pages use sentences or headings?
2   Look at the contents page opposite and use it to answer the following questions.
    a   How many **chapters** are there in the book?
    b   What is the book about? Make up a title.
    c   Where can you find out about sea mammals and birds?
    d   Where do you think you can find information on pollution?
    e   What's on pages 42 to 46?

Tip

Most books are divided into chapters. A chapter is a section of a book.

Unit 2 Going deep

Contents

Planet ocean	6	28	Kelp jungles	
Salty sea	8	30	Frozen feast	
Undersea landscape	10	32	Deep oceans	
Tides and waves	12	34	Ocean mysteries	
Weather-making sea	14	36	Studying the sea	
Living history	16	38	All fished out	
Fish rule	18	40	What a waste	
Ocean mammals	20	42	Projects	
Super sea-birds	22	44	Projects	
Who eats whom?	24	46	Projects	
Coral reef	26	48	Index	

3 Use the index to find further details in the same book.

a On which pages will you find information on dolphins?

b Which chapters will these pages be in?

c If you were looking for information on shells, would this book help you?

d Is there information in this book that will help you with your Collector's Card topics?

Index

birds 22–23, 38	manta rays 35
black smokers 11	plankton 7, 24, 25, 34, 35
coasts 12. 13	
coral 26, 27	octopuses 7
currents 14, 15	oil 40
Dead Sea 8	otters 29
deep oceans 7, 32–33	rain 14, 15
	salt 7–8
divers 37	sea-lions 29
dolphins 21, 31, 38	sea slugs 27, 42
dugongs 21	sea-urchins 28, 29
El Niño 15	seaweed 28
fish 16, 18–19, 26, 30, 32, 34, 38, 39, 44	sharks 18, 24, 38
	shipwrecks 37
fishing 38–39	starfish 45
food chains 24, 25	submersibles 37
islands, 11	tides 12–13
jellyfish 7, 46	turtles 35–38
krill 31	volcanoes 9, 11

B Work with key words and phrases.

1 Are any of the headings on the index page full sentences? How can you tell?

2 In your own words, explain the difference between:

> a sentence   a key word   a phrase

C Complete your reading log for the extracts from the sea life information book. Write a comment about whether you'd enjoy reading the book.

Session 4 Ordering information   **29**

5 Words in context

A — Identify words in their context.

1 With your talk partner discuss a possible meaning for each made-up word in **bold**. Replace each word with a real verb.
   a The fish **plumsed** right out of the water.
   b The delighted fishermen **boogled** plenty of fish.
   c We **splonched** into the cold, icy water.
   d In the storm the ship **cabooshed** into the iceberg.
   e The ship **galooped** to the bottom of the sea.

Did you know?
Sometimes you can work out the meaning of a word from the way it is used. This is called the 'context' of the word.

Tip
A verb is a word that describes an action.

Any volunteers? Who'd like to try out their nonsense word sentence on the class?

2 Have fun making up your own nonsense words in a sentence! Decide what you want your word to mean and use it in a sentence to see if your talk partner can work out the meaning from the context.

B — Read the introduction opposite and then answer the questions in your notebooks.

1 What is the purpose of this introduction?
2 Do you think you would find it at the front or the back of the book?
3 Can you think of a suitable title for this book?
4 Write a definition for each of the blue highlighted words without using a dictionary.
5 How many chapters does the book have?
6 What topics are covered?
7 Who is the book aimed at? How can you tell?
8 Could you use it to research information for your Collector's Cards?

Why not check your definitions in a dictionary after you've finished? Were you right?

30 Unit 2 Going deep

Do you enjoy nature? For those who **venture** out, nature offers a world of endless wonder and discovery. Consider this book your guide to many adventures and lots of fun. All you need is **curiosity**, patience and an open mind and you'll be surprised at what you find … oh, and don't forget your magnifying glass!

- In **chapter 1** you'll be introduced to our **unique** world, planet Earth, and find out why it is the only planet that can sustain life.
- **Chapter 2** is all about the **diversity** of life and how animals are grouped according to their different characteristics.
- **Chapter 3** explores different **habitats**. You'll learn about life in the sea, the desert, the jungle, the Arctic and even your back yard!
- **Chapter 4** deals with pollution and the effects of human activity on the Earth.

The nature adventure starts here but when and how it ends is up to you!

C Complete your reading log for the introduction. Which part of the book appeals to you most?

D Choose one of these books and write a short introduction. Use the title to imagine what it is about and the different chapters that you might find. Make notes with key words to plan your first draft.

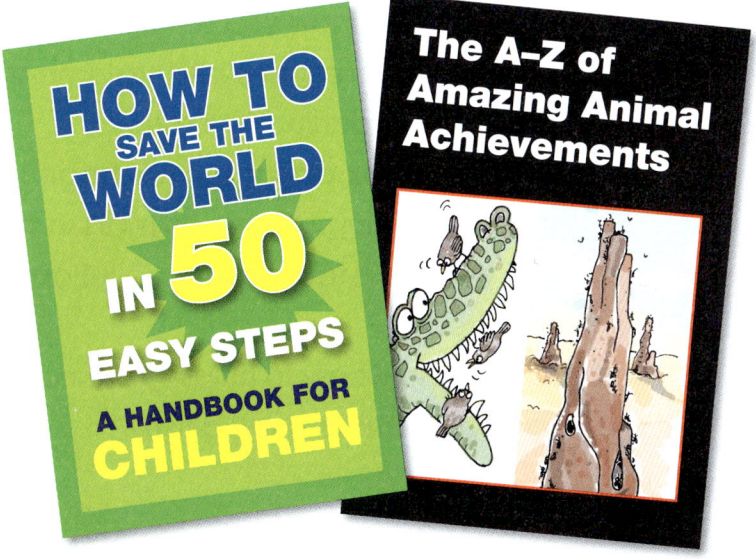

HOW TO SAVE THE WORLD IN 50 EASY STEPS
A HANDBOOK FOR CHILDREN

The A–Z of Amazing Animal Achievements

Session 5 Words in context

6 Work with sentences

A Revise sentences with different endings.
1 Sort these sentences into statements, questions and commands.
   a You really should read this book!
   b This book was very helpful.
   c Can I borrow that book for my project on fish?
   d I can highly recommend this book on oceans and seas.
   e Return it as soon as possible.
2 Re-read the introduction on the previous page and find an example of:
   a a command with an exclamation
   b a statement
   c a question.
3 Which type of sentence is the most common in the introduction? Can you tell why?

Language focus

A sentence **ends** with:
- a full stop (for statements)

or
- a question mark (for questions)

or
- an exclamation mark (for exclamations and some commands).

B Write statements from the text.
1 In the introduction text on the previous page find a statement that means:
   a It's always fun to learn about nature.
   b You'll learn many things when you go outside.
   c This book will show you where to start.
2 Change these sentences into statements. Start with the underlined words.
   a Read this book about animal habitats.
   b Find information on sea animals in this book.
   c Can you learn to measure pollution in ponds and streams?
   d Do you know how to classify animals?
   e Can you learn to draw a fish?

Tip

A command can also act as an exclamation.

Come here! Stand still! Hurry up!

Unit 2 Going deep

7 Revise and use sentences, phrases and key words

A Use this information to revise and remember what you should know about sentences.

Language focus

A **sentence** is a group of words with a verb, which makes complete sense. It begins with a capital letter and ends with a full stop.

Sentences are used to:
- answer questions
- form paragraphs and stories
- explain things
- provide information about something.

A **phrase** is a group of words that form part of a sentence. Phrases are useful for writing headings and making notes.

A **key word** is the main word in a sentence or paragraph. It summarises the main point of the sentence or paragraph.

1 Match the sentences from an introduction text to the headings from a contents page.

Introduction text – full sentences	Contents page – headings
You will discover how to group sea animals.	Keeping fish
Learn about how to keep fish in a tank.	Unusual animal habitats
This book will help you explore unusual places where animals live.	Making a toy octopus
You can find out how to make a toy octopus.	Classification of sea animals

Session 7 Revise and use sentences, phrases and key words

2 Make up your own sentences using the words in each of these headings.
   a Life in rock pools   b Collecting shells   c Unique habitats
3 Now use key words and phrases to write four chapter headings.
   a In Chapter 1 you will be introduced to our **unique** world.
   b Chapter 2 is all about the **diversity** of life.
   c Chapter 3 explores different **habitats** – places where things live.
   d Chapter 4 deals with pollution and human activity on our planet.
4 Use your headings to design your own contents page.

8 Summarise the main idea

A Are you ready to summarise?
In this session you'll learn to summarise and write notes about a unique sea creature!

Tip

Summarising helps you check that you understand the main idea of what you've read or heard.

… so we touched down smoothly last Saturday at exactly 11a.m. and just two hours later we were eating a seafood lunch on the beach! We spent the next two days skiing, snorkelling, boating and surfing. It was so cool, we had unlimited time on the jet skis and …

So what did she say about her holiday?

She went away for a long weekend and had a great time!

34 Unit 2 Going deep

1. Listen to the text.
   a. Describe the tone: formal, friendly, serious, light-hearted, informative.
   b. Who is it written for? How can you tell?
   c. Recall five facts from the text without looking!
2. Read through the text. Describe the layout and the features. What type of text is it?

> **Did you know?**
> Headings don't have to be sentences, but they can be!

Sea Stars

What are sea stars?

Sea stars are commonly known as starfish. Although they have this name and they live in the sea they are not fish at all! They don't have gills or scales or fins like fish. They also move very differently. Starfish eat, sleep and move about in rock pools or on the ocean floor.

Interesting facts:
Starfish can live to be 35 years old!
Starfish have no brain and no blood.

What do they look like?

Starfish are easy to recognise – they look like stars! There are over 2000 species of different colours, shapes and sizes. Most have five 'arms' or sections arranged around a central disk. They have a tough, bony surface covered in spines and a soft underside. They don't have eyes like ours; instead they have an eye spot at the end of each arm. If you look closely you might see a tiny red spot. This helps the starfish to sense light and dark but it cannot see any detail.

Interesting fact:
Some starfish have 10 or 20 arms.
The sun starfish has up to 40 arms!

Session 8 Summarise the main idea   35

How do they move?

If you gently turn a starfish over you will see hundreds of tiny, muscular, tube 'feet'. With these tiny suction feet the starfish crawls along – quicker than you'd think!

> **Interesting fact:**
> The tiny tube feet are filled with sea water.

How do they protect themselves?

Starfish have to protect themselves from being eaten by birds, fish and other sea creatures such as sea otters. If they sense danger they can move and hide under rocks but if that doesn't work, a starfish can 'drop' an arm to get away! Don't worry – a starfish has a unique ability to grow a new arm! It takes about a year to grow back.

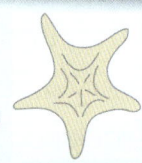

> **Interesting fact:**
> A starfish can grow a whole new starfish from just one arm and a piece of the middle disk.

What and how do they eat?

Starfish feed on clams, mussels, snails, barnacles and small fish. They use their arms and feet to hold their prey and pry the shells open. On their underside they have a tiny mouth.

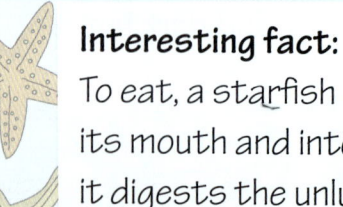

> **Interesting fact:**
> To eat, a starfish must push its stomach through its mouth and into the shell of its prey where it digests the unlucky animal before sliding its stomach back into its own body!

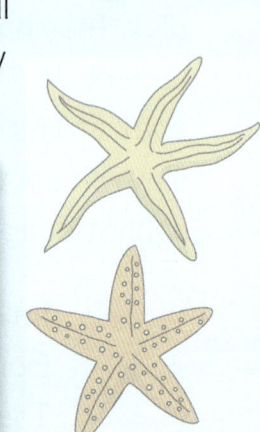

a galaxy of starfish
a herd of sea horses
a flurry of octopuses
a plantation of sea anemones

a pod of whales
a school of fish
a shiver of sharks
a cast of crabs

Have fun with collective nouns! Learn these unusual collective nouns and use them to impress your family!

B With your talk partner, make a mind map in your notebook.

1 Rewrite the headings from the *Sea Stars* passage using key words and phrases (e.g. How do they move? = Moving about).
2 Begin your mind map by writing the main topic in the middle. Then start adding your ideas.

Tip

Stick to essential key words and phrases.

C Now practise writing out information from your mind map notes.

1 Design five more Collector's Cards to add to your collection. Write an interesting heading for each card.
2 Write an interesting bit of information to go with each heading.

Any volunteers? Who'd like to share their favourite card with the class?

How did I do?

- Did I summarise information in a few key words and phrases on my mind map?
- Did I write full sentences from my mind map notes?

D Complete your reading log for the *Sea Stars* text. Write a comment to say whether you would enjoy reading more of it.

Session 8 Summarise the main idea

37

9 Looking at tenses

Verbs can change to show whether we are talking about the past, the present or the future. This is called the **tense**.

Tip

A verb describes an action or state of being e.g.
I **swim** in the sea.
or
I **am swimming** in the sea.

A Sometimes a verb is only one word (simple verb) and sometimes a verb is made up of groups of words, which help to show the tense of the verb.

1 Read through the *Sea Stars* text and identify ten simple verbs.
2 Here are some simple present tense verbs from the *Sea Stars* text.

> find   see   helps   grow   sleep

Write down the simple past and future tense of each one.

find › found › will find

B Sometimes sentences use more than one tense.

1 Which tenses have been used in these sentences and why? The verbs have been underlined.
   a If you <u>turn</u> a starfish over you <u>will see</u> hundreds of tiny, tube 'feet'.
   b If you <u>look</u> closely you <u>will see</u> a tiny red spot.
   c If a starfish '<u>drops</u>' an arm it <u>will grow</u> a new one in a year.
2 Write sentences using the present and future tense. Use these sentence starters to get going. One verb is underlined.
   Use a second verb in a different tense.
   a <u>Handle</u> a starfish carefully or …
   b A starfish <u>will hide</u> if …
   c If you <u>look</u> in a rock pool …

10 Work with connectives

A Connectives are linking words that are used to link sentences and paragraphs.

Did you know?

Some useful connectives are:

and, but, as well as, however, therefore, if, although, where, nevertheless, because

1 Read through the *Sea Stars* text with your talk partner and find examples of connectives.

Tip

Sometimes a connective can appear at the beginning of a sentence – look out for sentences that begin with *If*, *But* or *Although*.

B Use connectives from the list above to link the following sentences together.
   a Starfish have 'arms'. Starfish have 'feet'.
   b Starfish protect themselves. Starfish are in danger of being eaten by birds and fish.
   c Starfish cannot see details. Starfish can sense light and dark.

Tip

You don't have to repeat the word *starfish* when you join these sentences. You can use *they* instead.

11 and 12 Collect information for an oral presentation

A You've read about starfish and designed Collector's Cards. Now you're going to prepare to tell your class about a sea creature of your choice.

1 Choose a sea creature that you find interesting. Here are some ideas:

> jellyfish   sperm whale   needlefish   seahorse

2 What would you like to know about your sea creature? Think of five questions and write them in your notebook.

3 Where will you look for information on your topic? What is available in your school or home for you to use?

4 Collect information. Under each of your questions, write key words and phrases to help you remember the main points of information.

B Present your information at a sea life exhibition.

1 Create a poster to display about your sea creature.
- Find or draw a picture or diagram of your sea creature.
- Arrange your questions, key words and phrases around the picture in a way that will help you remember what you want to say.

2 Practise presenting your information, using the key points on your poster as a reminder.

3 Display your posters to make a class exhibition and enjoy listening to each other's talks.

You're going to create a class exhibition about sea life and each give a short talk about your sea creatures!

Tip
Remember to use neat, joined-up handwriting to present your work.

40   Unit 2 Going deep

3 Mind pictures

Before people had radio, television, computers or phones, poems and songs were a major form of entertainment! In this unit you'll learn about ancient riddles and rhymes and find unusual ways to describe ordinary things. You'll write your own poems and discover how good you are at painting mind pictures.

Vocabulary to learn and use:
literal, figurative, poem, poetry, kenning, riddle, rhyme, rhythm, syllables

1 Use your imagination

A Read these two descriptions of the sun.

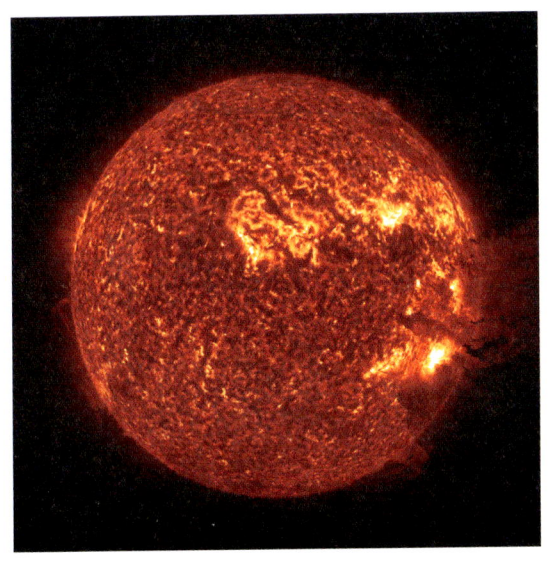

A ball of fire around which Earth orbits.

A fiery furnace, showering Earth with light and life.

1 Use the dictionary definitions to decide which description is literal and which is figurative.
2 Discuss with a talk partner which description you prefer. Explain why.
3 Invent another figurative description of the sun together.

Any volunteers? Who'd like to share their figurative description with the class?

figurative *adj.* not exact; using imaginative or exaggerated description
literal *adj.* precise; meaning exactly what is said, not exaggerated

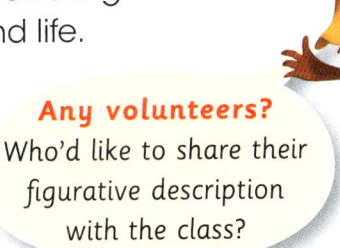

Session 1 Use your imagination 41

B 💬 A **kenning** is a type of figurative language popular in Old English and Norse poetry. A kenning is a descriptive phrase that tells you about something without saying what it is – like a riddle or a puzzle.

Did you know?

Old English (or Anglo Saxon) was spoken in England between the 5th and 11th centuries. They called their language Englisc.

Vikings is an Old Norse word meaning explorers, traders and warriors who travel by ship.

Old English and Norse stories about heroes and battles were often told in long poems known as **epics**. Poets used kennings to add variety and conjure up vivid mind pictures.

1 Use your imagination to discuss what these kennings are describing.

> whale road   earth-walker   iron shower
> world candle   storm of swords   sea stallion

2 Sometimes kennings were combined to extend the images. Discuss what a *stallion of the whale road* could be.

3 Invent a kenning for an aeroplane.

Unit 3 Mind pictures

C 💬 People in Old English and Norse times enjoyed inventing and guessing riddles.

> ### Language focus
> **Poetic technique** Alliteration was popular in Old English poetry and kennings; it helped add dramatic effect. Alliteration is when the same letter or sound at the beginning of several words is repeated for effect. It is especially useful when poems are said aloud: *Round the rugged rock, the ragged rascal ran.*

1 Work in a group to solve these ancient riddles.

A wonder on the wave
Water became bone.

Glittering points
That downward thrust,
Sparkling spears
That never rust.

Tip
Close your eyes and think of these kenning mind pictures!

2 Identify an example of alliteration in both riddles.

D 💬 Riddles can be challenging to create as well as to solve.

1 Talk about how this modern kennings riddle was developed.
2 Think of a kenning to add to describe an ostrich's long neck.
3 Put the riddle together in any order you like and practise saying it aloud.

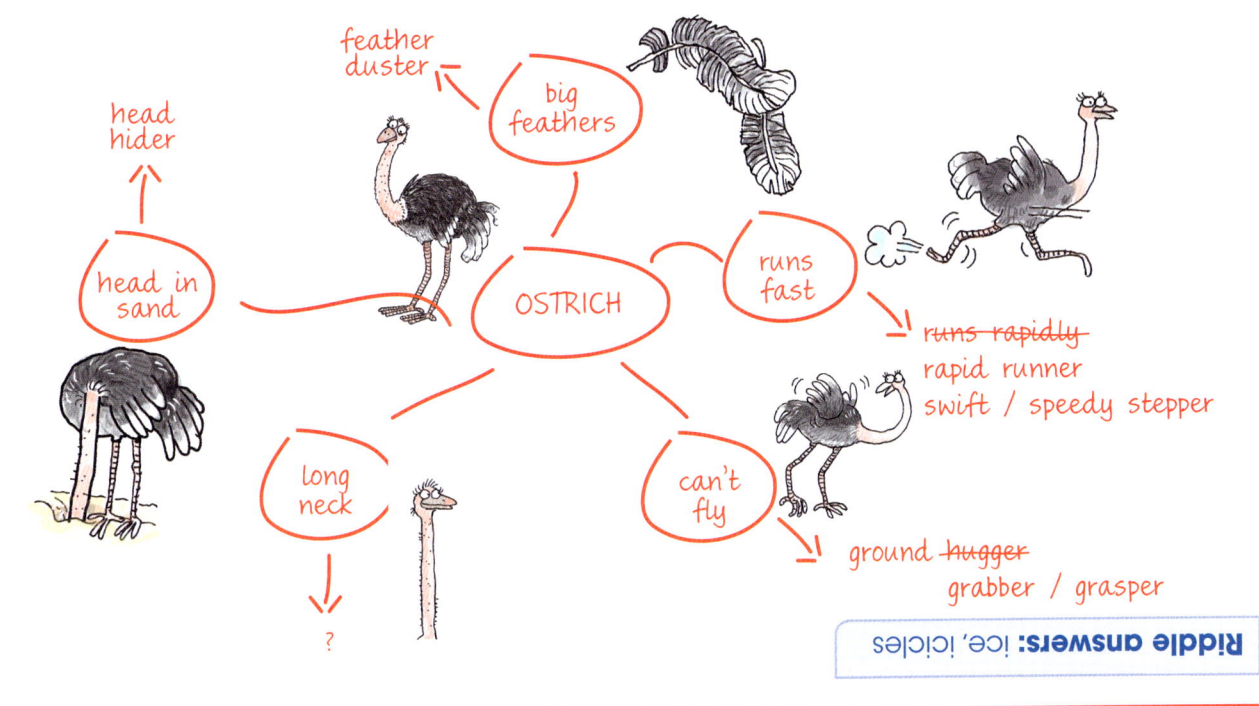

feather duster
head hider
big feathers
head in sand
OSTRICH
runs fast
long neck
can't fly
?

~~runs rapidly~~
rapid runner
swift / speedy stepper

ground ~~hugger~~
grabber / grasper

Riddle answers: ice, icicles

Session 1 Use your imagination   43

E Follow the same process to develop your own animal riddle composed of kennings.

1. In your group, pick an animal and come up with four or five mind pictures of it.
2. Use a thesaurus or a dictionary to help you choose unusual, descriptive words or words that use alliteration to create the kennings; like *swift stepper* or *ground grasper*.
3. Practise and present the riddle for the class to guess your animal.

Tip
Focus on the rhythm when you say it aloud.

F Record reading the kennings riddles in your reading log. Note what you thought about them.

2 Meet a modern poet who uses kennings

A Work with a talk partner to read and discuss the kenning poems opposite.

1. Suggest why the poet chose these images.
2. What clues suggest he is a modern poet?
3. How does the layout of the poem without commas indicate a list?
4. What two meanings could *Tall story weaver* have?

Tip
A **colon** (:) can be used to introduce a list.

A **comma** (,) usually separates items in a list.

An **exclamation mark** (!) tells you to put emphasis on words or sentences.

B Explore rhyme and rhythm as you read the poems aloud.

1. The lines ending in **er** rhyme in pairs.
   a. Identify the underlined vowel sound in each pair of rhymes.
   b. Is the underlined sound short or long?
   c. Do any of the rhyming pairs of words share the same sound as another pair?
   d. Do any of the rhyming pairs have the same underlined letter pattern as another pair, but a different sound?

W<u>ea</u>ver – f<u>e</u>ver
t<u>e</u>ller – y<u>e</u>ller
w<u>ea</u>rer – b<u>ea</u>rer
b<u>a</u>nisher – v<u>a</u>nisher
m<u>o</u>wer – s<u>o</u>wer
h<u>u</u>gger – m<u>u</u>gger
squ<u>a</u>sher – n<u>o</u>sher
st<u>ea</u>ler – h<u>ea</u>ler
t<u>i</u>ghter – r<u>i</u>ghter

Unit 3 Mind pictures

Dad

He's a:

Tall story weaver
Full of fib fever
Bad joke teller
Ten **decibel** yeller
Baggy clothes wearer
Pocket money bearer
Nightmare banisher
Hurt heart vanisher

Bear hugger
Biscuit mugger
Worry squasher
Noisy **nosher**
Lawn mower
Smile sower

Football mad
Fashion sad
Not half bad
So glad I had
My
Dad!

Mum

She's a:

Sadness stealer
Cut-knee healer
Hug-me-tighter
Wrongness righter
Gold star carer
Chocolate sharer
 (well, sometimes!)

Hamster feeder
Bedtime reader
Great game player
Night fear slayer
Treat dispenser
Naughty sensor (how
 come she always
 knows?)

She's my
Never glum,
Constant chum
Second to none
We're under her thumb!
Mum!

Andrew Fusek Peters

decibel *n.* a unit for measuring how loud a sound is
nosher *n.* eater (*informal*)

Session 2 Meet a modern poet who uses kennings

Did you know?

Rhythm and rhyme have been used in poetry for thousands of years. The ancient Greeks thought they made poems and stories easier to remember. Most people couldn't read so they memorised poems and passed them on orally.

Tip

- A syllable is a sound unit or beat in a word. You can clap your hands once saying *Dad* and twice saying *fa/ther*. Dad has one syllable; *father* has two syllables.
- Each word has one stressed syllable (long). **DAD** is one stressed syllable; **FA**/*ther* has the stress on the first syllable not the second.

2 Discuss the rhythm effect created by the syllables in the last word on each line of the poems on the previous page.
    a How many syllables does the last word in each line have?
    b How is this emphasised in the layout of the poem?

Language focus

Poetic technique
A **stanza** is a group of lines of poetry forming a unit.
Verse means words that belong together as poetry – a line or two, a stanza or an entire poem. Sometimes *verse* is used in place of **stanza**.
Each of the poems above has three main stanzas.

3 Discuss the rhymes in the last stanza of each poem.
    a Identify the vowel sound in the rhymes.
    b Why do you think the poet chose these rhyming sounds for each final stanza?

C **AZ** Explore the effect of alliteration in the poems.

1 *Wrongness righter* is one of the kennings describing Mum. Discuss whether this is alliteration and share a reason with the class.
2 Identify other examples of alliteration in the poems.

D Practise reading the poems aloud. Focus on pace, rhythm and flow and expressive body language.

1 Give each other feedback on reading aloud skills.
2 Present the poems to each other or the class.

Challenge yourself:
Choose one or more kennings from each poem with no alliteration and rewrite them using alliteration, e.g.
Tall story weaver → Tall tale teller.

3 Plan and write a kenning poem

A **AZ** Write a kenning poem about a friend or a relative.

1 Choose a person important to you and visualise what you like about them. What do they do? What do they enjoy? What are they like?

Session 3 Plan and write a kenning poem

2   Write down key words and phrases for each mind picture.

carpet creeper
picture painter
crafty card dealer

3   Think of a kenning for each idea or characteristic – following the pattern of adjectives, nouns and verbs in the different stanzas.

   a   Write six to eight lines. Each line must have at least three syllables with a clear rhythm.
   b   Each pair of lines must rhyme.
   c   With a talk partner work to improve your kennings.
   d   Choose more powerful verbs: noisy ~~eater~~ nosher; picture ~~painter~~ sketcher
   e   Use alliteration in at least one kenning: ~~picture~~ speedy sketcher
   f   Present and illustrate your poem in an imaginative way.

Adjective	Noun	Verb	+ er
crafty	card picture	deal paint	er er

Tip

When you present your work, use joined-up handwriting, taking care with tall and short letters and letters that go below the line. It helps make your work easy and enjoyable to read.

Any volunteers? Who'd like to share their kenning?

How did I do?

- Did I include alliteration and rhythm?
- Did I write good clues that people could guess the answers to?

Unit 3 Mind pictures

4 What is a colour?

Are there any other names for my colour?

A 📖 💬 Questions are a great way to start thinking about something ordinary in imaginative ways. Find a literal or factual answer from a dictionary and let it spark your ideas.

What does colour mean?

1 Look up *colour* in the dictionary. How many definitions do you find?

   a Use a thesaurus to build a word bank in your notebook for your favourite colour.

   b Use questions to help you plan ideas and images to use in a colour poem. Use your notebook plan and colours.

   c Share your ideas with the class and make suggestions to each other for colour images and mind pictures.

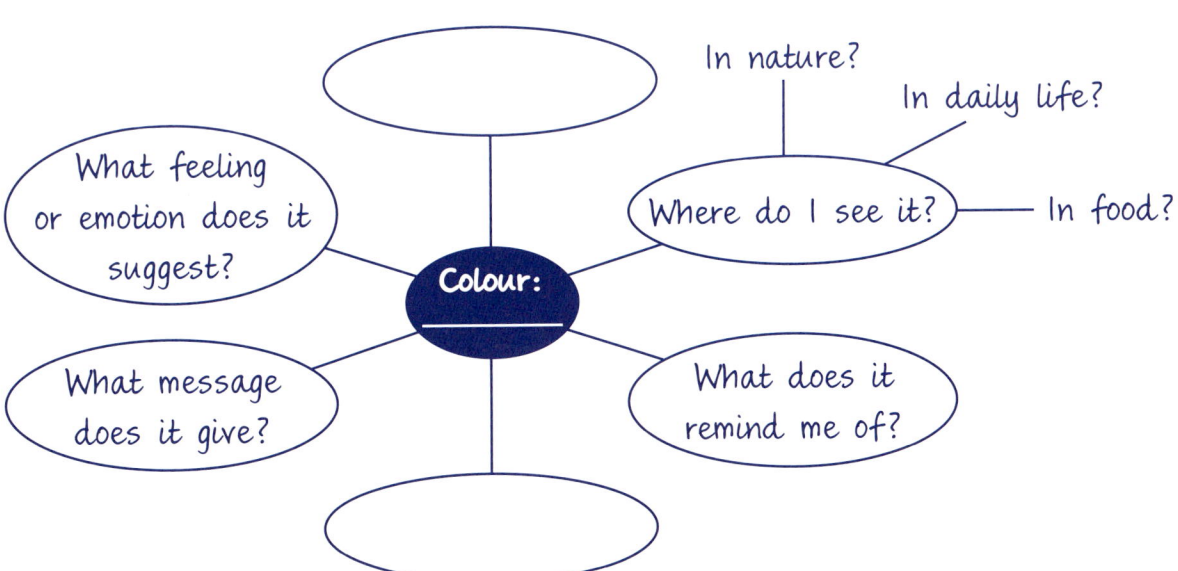

Tip
Add questions of your own too!

Mind map around **Colour:**
- In nature?
- In daily life?
- Where do I see it? — In food?
- What does it remind me of?
- What message does it give?
- What feeling or emotion does it suggest?

B 📖 Listen to a 'red' poem for inspiration. Close your eyes and imagine different shades of the colour as you listen.

Session 4 What is a colour? 49

What is red?

Red is a sunset
Blazing and bright.
Red is feeling brave
With all your might.
5 Red is a sunburn
Spot on your nose,
Sometimes red
Is a red, red rose.
Red squiggles out
10 When you cut your hand.
Red is a brick and
The sound of a band.
Red is a hotness
You get inside
15 When you're embarrassed
And want to hide.
Fire-cracker, fire engine
Fire-flicker red –
And when you're angry
20 Red runs through your head.

Red is a lipstick,
Red is a shout,
Red is a signal
That says: "Watch out!"
25 Red is a great big
Rubber ball.
Red is the giant-est
Color of all.
Red is a show-off
30 No doubt about it –
But can you imagine
Living without it?
Mary O'Neill

color ng American spelling of *colour*

Unit 3 Mind pictures

C Talk about the poem in a group. What did you enjoy?

1. List the 'red mind pictures' in lines 1–8. Do you like them?
2. What is the red that *squiggles out* in line 9?
3. The images in lines 17–24 are loosely linked. Which abstract noun links the images best: happiness, danger, fear, sorrow, caution, bravery, love?
4. Suggest a reason why red is called *a show-off* in line 29.
5. Add one more red mind picture for your group. Make sure it is a sentence.

Tip

Remember to use examples from the poem in your responses!

5 Focus on poetic technique

A When you write a poem, you have to decide what to write about and how you will do it (poetic techniques).

1. Re-read the poem *What is Red?* closely and jot down notes about techniques the poet has used. Use the **Poem box** questions to help you.
2. Review your earlier plan for a colour poem in your notebook and add a couple of poetic techniques you could use.

Poem box

How many stanzas and lines do I have?	*One, two, three or more?*
Do I have rhymes?	*I'm a poet although I don't know it, but no rhymes are OK too!*
Is there a pattern?	*AABB, ABAB, ABCB …*
Can you feel a rhythm in my syllables?	*DA-dum DA-dum DA-dum …*
Do you hear alliteration?	*Poems paint perfect pictures.*
What about repetition?	*Repetition creates a special effect.*
What mood or effect do I create?	*Mysterious, thoughtful, funny?*
How do I look?	*A verse, a swirl, a colour, a curl?*

B Questions create mind pictures too.

Tip: What? Why? When? Where? How? Who? are useful question words.

1 What two features show that the poem title, *What is Red?*, is a question?
   a Invent titles for colour poems using other question words.
   b Listen to your teacher read the poem *Who Knows?* Which question words have been used?
   c Add a question using *when*, *why* or *what* to the poem following the same feel and flow, and the same theme.

Who knows?

Who knows
How many stars
Are in the roof of the sky?
How many fishes
In the deep seas?
How many people
In the whole wide world?
Who knows
Where, every evening
The sun flees to?
Where the moon lights up?
Where dawn starts,
Where the endless horizon ends.
Who knows? ... Who knows?

Fatou Ndiaye Sow

Unit 3 Mind pictures

C Complete your reading log for the poems *Dad, Mum, What is Red?* and *Who knows?* Say whether you enjoyed reading them, and which one you enjoyed the most.

6 Write a colour poem

A Use your plan to write a colour poem.
- Include at least one question in the title or the poem.
- Paint colour mind pictures using images to answer the questions in your planning.
- Use your word bank of synonyms to select interesting colour words.
- Include one or two poetic techniques like repetition, rhyme, rhythm or alliteration.

B Read your poem to a talk partner with their eyes closed. Give each other feedback on the mind pictures and images in your poems.

> **Tip**
> What is the poem's mood? Does it make you think or laugh, or does it send shivers down your spine?

C Present your poem in a creative way.
You could illustrate it, do a computer presentation with images or set it to music that suits your colour.

D Have fun showing and performing your poems to each other.

Let's have a poetry party!

Session 6 Write a colour poem 53

4 Just imagine

Some stories make you feel the events could really have happened. Other stories need you to use your imagination and enter a world where even the animals can talk. In this chapter, you will meet some interesting animal characters from past and present. You will read a blurb and develop a storyboard for a fable.

Vocabulary to learn and use:
blurb, contraction, legacy, inherit, inheritance, foist, build-up, climax, resolution, apostrophe, possession

1 Read a blurb

A Choosing the right book to read can be difficult. You have to know what you like but also be prepared to try new genres. Reading the **blurb** on the back of a book can help you decide.

1 With a talk partner read this information about blurbs.

- A blurb is like an advertisement on the back of the book to make you want to read it.

- A blurb gives you a taste of what the book is like – it usually includes an extract from the book.

- A blurb tells you just enough to show what sort of book it is, without giving too much away and spoiling the storyline.

- Blurbs sometimes include a review or quote from someone who has read it.

Unit 4 Just imagine

2 Read the back cover of a fiction book from the class library. Does its blurb match the comments on the previous page?

3 Compare the comments with the blurb for *Harry's Mad* by Dick King-Smith.

This book will keep you laughing from cover to cover!

"Has Great Uncle George left Harry something?" asked Mrs Holdsworth.

"Yes, he has."

5 "His fortune?" cried Harry.

"His fortune?" said his father. "No such luck, Harry. The old boy didn't have a lot of money, and what he did have he's left to his

10 university library. No, he's left you what appears to have been his most cherished possession."

"What's that?" said Harry.

"His parrot."

15 Having a Grey African parrot **foisted** upon him all the way from America isn't Harry's idea of a decent **legacy**. He'd been dreaming of untold riches and

20 then all he got was this boring old parrot! But when Madison introduces himself in perfect American, Harry discovers that the parrot has hidden talents.

25 For Mad is not just a chatty beak. He is an ace at crosswords and board games, especially Monopoly, a fund of useful information and a natural mimic –

30 he can impersonate all the family with ease. Even Harry's homework improves under Mad's expert – and interesting – tuition and soon the whole family is wondering

35 what they ever did without him. Unfortunately, they are about to find out.

The escapades of Harry and Mad send more than feathers flying, creating a ripping yarn, fizzing with Dick King-Smith's delightful, outrageous humour.

Books for your Children

foist *v.* force someone to have or experience something they do not want

Tip

When someone has died, we say they 'leave' their possessions to people rather 'give' them and what they leave is called a **legacy**. When people receive possessions from someone who has died, we say they 'inherit' those possessions.

Session 1 Read a blurb   55

B Complete your reading log for the *Harry's Mad* blurb and comment on whether you might enjoy reading the story.

> **Did you know?**
> Dick King-Smith was a farmer and a teacher before becoming a writer and many of his amusing animal stories are based on his farming experiences.

2 Harry's Mad

A Discuss *Harry's Mad* in a group.

1 The word bank shows synonyms for the adjective *funny*. Starting with *funny*, order the adjectives in increasing intensity according to how funny you think they are (e.g. *side-splitting* implies something is funnier than *amusing*). Share your order with the class.

> funny   humorous   hilarious   comical   amusing   side-splitting
> whacky   rib-tickling   entertaining   riotous   hysterical

2 Select one of the adjectives you predict would apply to *Harry's Mad*.
3 Choose the front cover that best suits the book. Use evidence from the blurb to back up your opinion.

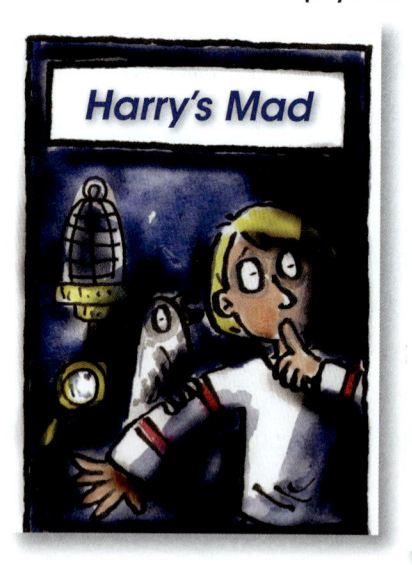

4 Complete this sentence to summarise the evidence in the blurb suggesting that the book will be funny.

The blurb suggests the book will be funny because …

B With a talk partner, jot down notes to answer the questions about the characters.

Tip: Remember to look at the dialogue!

1. Which characters are mentioned in the blurb?
2. Who do you think are the main characters in the book? Choose one of the options below and give reasons based on evidence from the blurb and your own knowledge of stories.

Harry and Great Uncle George	Mad and Mrs Holdsworth	Harry and Mad

3. What did the blurb tell you about Mad?
4. Do you think Harry will end up being pleased that Great Uncle George left him Mad rather than lots of money? Why?
5. Which legacy would you prefer?

What do I look like?
How do I speak?
What can I do?

3 Understand the plot

A Most stories follow a recipe with a few different ingredients each time to add interest. Getting the recipe right is important!

INTRODUCTION
Characters and settings

PLOT:
Build-up
Events that set the scene for an issue to be resolved.

Complication/Climax
A complication or exciting event occurs.
What will happen is unclear.

Resolution
The issue is resolved.

ENDING
Reflection by a character or narrator.
Happy, sad or ambiguous.

Session 3 Understand the plot 57

1 The events in the *Harry's Mad* plot got muddled. Use the story recipe on page 57 to help you order the events in the most likely sequence.

> Mad escapes from the thief's house but is lost in London.

> Harry's parents find out Mad's secret.

> Mad is stolen by a thief.

> Harry finds Mad in Trafalgar Square – his favourite destination on the board game.

> The family enjoy discovering the amazing things Mad is able to do.

> Harry inherits a parrot called Mad from Great Uncle George, and discovers it can talk like a person.

Any volunteers? Who can match the events to the *introduction, build-up, complication/climax* and *resolution*?

B The ending of a story often contains a reflection or events to show life is back to normal after the problem or complication has been resolved.

1 Use these story notes to explore ideas for how the story ends.

> – While Mad is still missing, Dad buys Harry another parrot, known as 'Fweddy', that cannot talk like Mad.
> – The final words of the story are: '*Call me Dad*', said Harry's Mad.

2 Try out your ideas on a talk partner and listen to their comments.
3 Review your ideas and write a short ending to the story, leading up to the final words. Write mainly in the past tense except for dialogue.
4 Check your spelling carefully.
5 Write your story ending in neat, joined-up writing so that it is easy to check and read aloud.
6 Read your ending aloud to your talk partner to check for sense and missing words.

4 Read more about Harry and Mad

A Read this extract from *Harry's Mad* by Dick King-Smith in groups of three: narrator, Harry and Mad.

Harry's Mad

Harry took a deep breath. A hundred times, he said to himself, I'll say it a hundred times. He leant forward till his lips were almost against the wire
5 bars of the cage, as close as possible to where he thought the bird's ear must be, and, speaking slowly and clearly, as you would to a foreigner or someone rather deaf, he said,
10 "My … name … is … Madison."

The parrot scratched the side of his bare, scaly face with one foot.

"If you say so, buddy," he said clearly, "but that would be a
15 remarkable coincidence. Seeing that my name is Madison also."

Harry's mouth fell open. He felt amazement, embarrassment, wild excitement, all at the same time.
20 "What's the matter?" said Madison pleasantly. "Cat got your tongue?"

"You can talk?" said Harry at last in a kind of hoarse whisper.

"Uh-huh."
25 "Properly!"

"Sure. Mebbe a mite differently from you, seeing I was raised in America, but boy, I sure can talk."

"But … I thought parrots could
30 only say a few words."

"Depends on how well they've been taught. I've spent all my life with a **professor of linguistics**. Dead now, but what a guy!"
35 "Great Uncle George!"

"George Holdsworth was your great-uncle? You're a Holdsworth?"

"Yes. He left you to me. In his will."

"Gee!" he said. "That explains
40 it all. They shoved me in that box, drove me to the airport, and next thing I know, I'm at Heathrow. Madison Holdsworth, I said to myself, it's London Zoo for you, I guess.
45 Instead of which I'm back with the family. Boy, am I glad to be here!"

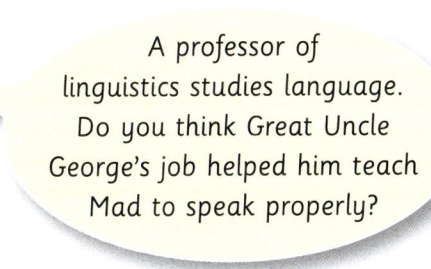

A professor of linguistics studies language. Do you think Great Uncle George's job helped him teach Mad to speak properly?

Session 4 Read more about Harry and Mad

Language focus

Countries often use different words to mean the same thing, for example:
friend – buddy; sweets – candy; holiday – vacation.
Many countries also adopt words into English from local languages.
In South Africa, *braai* means barbeque. The word comes from Afrikaans, one of the languages spoken in South Africa.
Braai, barbeque, barbecue, BBQ and *barbie* are all words for a social gathering and meal where food is cooked outdoors over an open grill or fire. What word do you use?

The words barbie and BBQ are different types of abbreviation. Can you see how?

1 Skim read the extract from *Harry's Mad* on page 59.
2 Discuss the main idea of the extract with a talk partner.
3 On your own, closely read the parts where Mad speaks. Does he use any words or expressions that are not used where you live?
4 *Mebbe* (line 26) is not a real word. Use the context to work out what English word it should be. Why do you think the author wrote *Mebbe*?
5 A *mite* is an unusual word meaning a *small but noticeable amount*. What word would be more commonly used where you live?
6 Scan the extract for informal words or expressions. Are they familiar to you? What would you say instead?

B Complete your reading log for the *Harry's Mad* extract. Are you enjoying the story?

Any volunteers? Who'd like to demonstrate Harry's body language and reaction when the parrot speaks?

5 Present a dramatic reading

Language focus

The speech marks show when Harry or Mad is speaking. Anything not inside the speech marks should be read by the narrator. If you are reading one of the characters, imagine how you would feel if it was you – it will help you sound convincing.

60 Unit 4 Just imagine

A Practise reading the extract in your group.
- Pay particular attention to the American words and expressions.
- Consider body language, actions and possible props to dramatise the reading.
- Use the new paragraphs to help you notice when a new person starts to speak.

1 Perform your extract to another group for feedback.
2 Listen to the feedback and review your performance as a group.

Tip

Remember these tips when you are practising your reading!
- Mad has an American accent (and sounds like a parrot).
- Harry is surprised and amazed to discover Mad talks so well.
- Read the words accurately from the script.
- Use the punctuation to make sense of the reading and add expression: commas, full stops, question marks and exclamation marks.
- Speak clearly and at an appropriate pace.

How did I do?
- Did I sound American?
- Did I speak clearly?
- Did my body language help?

Session 5 Present a dramatic reading

6 Check your understanding

A Answer these questions in your notebook, using textual evidence in your answers.

1 What is Mad's full name?
2 What three feelings did Harry have when Mad first spoke to him?
3 What body language showed Harry's feelings?
4 Where did Mad think he was being sent?
5 What words tell you Mad is pleased to be with Harry's family?
6 Why do you think Harry spoke to *Mad slowly and clearly, as you would to a foreigner or someone rather deaf*?
7 Write a short paragraph to describe how you might react if you came across an animal that could talk to you.

7 Work with adverbs

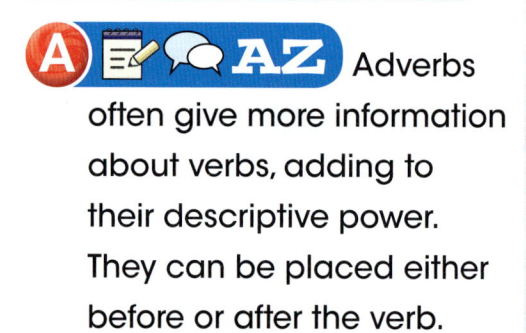

A Adverbs often give more information about verbs, adding to their descriptive power. They can be placed either before or after the verb.

Language focus

Regular adverbs are formed from adjectives and end in the suffix **ly**.
sad – sadly; happy – happily;
careful – carefully; amiable – amiably
Notice the spelling rule:
- Adjectives that end in **y** change **y** to **i** before adding the suffix **ly** (*pretty – prettily*).
- Adjectives ending in **ble**, drop the final **e** before adding the suffix **ly** (*terrible – terribly*).

1 Turn each of these adjectives into an adverb by adding the suffix **ly**.

> quick slow clear fair bad hungry cheeky
> hasty thankful skilful grateful

2 These adverbs were also formed from adjectives. Can you work out what the adjectives are?

> solidly softly loudly crazily lazily messily
> thoughtfully successfully gracefully

Unit 4 Just imagine

3 Discuss an appropriate adverb that could make each underlined verb more descriptive.

> slightly   nervously   tightly   gracefully   confidently   swiftly   fully

Harry <u>opened</u> the cage door (*adverb*), and the parrot (*adverb*) <u>leapt</u> out and up onto his shoulder. Mad <u>gripped</u> Harry's shoulder (*adverb*) making him <u>wince</u> (*adverb*). Mad then <u>walked</u> (*adverb*) down Harry's arm before (*adverb*) <u>stretching</u> out his wings and <u>flying</u> (*adverb*) across to the table.

4 Find an alternative adverb to replace each adverb ending in **ly** in the extract on page 59. Example,

... speaking slowly deliberately and clearly plainly, as you would to a foreigner or someone rather deaf.

Tip
Use a dictionary or a thesaurus to help you choose alternative adverbs.

8 Learn more about apostrophes

A Listen to your teacher re-read the extract from *Harry's Mad* and listen for any words that are contractions. Raise your hand when you hear one. Your teacher will pause for you to say the full words.

Language focus

Apostrophes

Apostrophes (') have two main jobs:

Contractions – to show where letters or sounds have been left out when words or sounds are combined or shortened:
cannot – can't; do not – don't; I will – I'll.
We use contractions when we speak but we usually use full words in formal writing.

Possession – to show when something belongs to someone or something:
the book that belongs to the boy > the boy's book.

Session 8 Learn more about apostrophes

1 Are the contractions in the extract used when someone speaks or in the narrator text? Why?
2 Rewrite the following phrases using an apostrophe to show possession.

> the cage of the parrot   the house belonging to the family
> the journey of the parrot   the parrot of Great Uncle George

3 Find these phrases in the extract and rewrite them without using the possessive form: *bird's ear, Harry's mouth*.
4 What do you think the title, *Harry's Mad*, means? Can you think of two possible meanings?

9 The Voyages of Doctor Dolittle

A 💬 The Doctor Dolittle stories are about a doctor who learns to talk to animals.
1 Skim over the Doctor Dolittle extract and discuss with a talk partner what the characters are talking about.
2 Discuss who appears to be telling the story: a boy (Tommy Stubbins), or Polynesia the parrot? Find evidence to support your answer.
3 Summarise the key points of the extract: characters, setting, main idea.

Did you know?
Although Hugh Lofting wrote the stories in the 1920s, they are set in Victorian England in the 1840s, so they are historical stories for two reasons.

> Old-fashioned books often used Roman numerals to number the chapters. What number chapter is VIII?

64 Unit 4 Just imagine

A nine-year-old boy named Tommy Stubbins, the **cobbler's** son, has discovered that Doctor Dolittle can talk to animals. While he is at the doctor's house, having breakfast and drying off in front of the fire, Tommy speaks to Polynesia, Doctor Dolittle's parrot friend from Africa.

Chapter VIII Are you a good noticer?

"Do you think I would ever be able to learn the language of the animals?" I asked, laying the plate upon the **hearth**.

"Well, it all depends," said Polynesia. "Are you clever at lessons?"

"I don't know," I answered, feeling rather ashamed. "You see, I've never been to school. My father is too poor to send me."

"Well," said the parrot, "I don't suppose you have really missed much to judge from what I have seen of school-boys. But listen: are you a good noticer? Do you notice things well? I mean, for instance, supposing you saw two cock-starlings on an apple-tree, and you only took one good look at them – would you be able to tell one from the other if you saw them again the next day?"

"I don't know," I said. "I've never tried."

"Well that," said Polynesia, brushing some crumbs off the corner of the table with her left foot, "that is what you call powers of observation – noticing the small things about birds and animals: the way they walk and move their heads and flip their wings; the way they sniff the air and twitch their whiskers and wiggle their tails. You have to notice all those little things if you want to learn animal language. For you see, lots of the animals hardly talk at all with their tongues; they use their breath or their tails or their feet instead. That is because many of them, in the **olden days** when lions and tigers were more plentiful, were afraid to make a noise for fear the savage creatures heard them. Birds, of course, didn't care; for they always had wings to fly away with. But that is the first thing to remember: being a good noticer is terribly important in learning animal language."

"It sounds pretty hard," I said.

"You'll have to be very patient," said Polynesia. "It takes a long time to say even a few words properly. But if you come here often I'll give you a few lessons myself. And once you get started you'll be surprised how fast you get on. It would indeed be a good thing if you could learn. Because then you could do some of the work for the Doctor – I mean the easier work, like bandaging and giving pills. Yes, yes, that's a good idea of mine. '**Twould** be a great thing if the poor man could get some help – and some rest. It is a scandal the way he works. I see no reason why you shouldn't be able to help him a great deal – that is, if you are really interested in animals."

"Oh, I'd love that!" I cried. "Do you think the Doctor would let me?"

Hugh Lofting

B Discuss with a talk partner and then write the answers in your notebook in neat, joined-up handwriting.

1 What does this extract tell you about school in those days?

> "Well, it all depends," said Polynesia. "Are you clever at lessons?"
> "I don't know," I answered, feeling rather ashamed. "You see, I've never been to school. My father is too poor to send me."

2 Why do you think Tommy felt ashamed?
3 How would you feel if you had never been able to go to school? Share your ideas in a few sentences.
4 According to Polynesia, what skills are needed to learn animal language and why?
5 Predict from your knowledge of stories whether the Doctor will let Tommy learn animal language.
6 Based on what Polynesia says, explain whether you would be good at learning animal language.

C Update your reading log to include the *The Voyages of Doctor Dolittle* and *Harry's Mad* extracts. Add your thoughts on the stories so far.

10 Focus on language

A The extract contains words and phrases that may be unfamiliar today. Did you notice any?

1 Discuss the meaning of the words shown in blue in the underlined phrases in the extract.

Tip
If you can't work out their meaning from the context, use a dictionary or another research method.

B Re-read the extract closely focusing on the verbs.

1 Find three examples of verbs in the main extract that show the story is narrated in the past tense.
2 Rewrite the contractions below in full.
"I **don't know**," I answered, feeling rather ashamed. "You **see**, I'**ve** never **been** to school. My **father's** too poor to send me."

Unit 4 Just imagine

3 Identify the verb tenses of the **underlined** verbs in the dialogue. What do you notice?

C Polynesia and Tommy ask each other a lot of questions but they don't always use question words in their questions.

1 Turn these questions from the extract into statements:
- Are you a good noticer?
- Do you think the Doctor would let me?

2 Turn these statements into questions:
- You are interested in animals.
- Polynesia is very patient.
- I can help the doctor.

For these ones, add *do* or *does*:
- You understand animal language.
- Animals like the Doctor.
- Tommy wants to learn animal language.

3 Discuss what happened to the verb when *does* was used.
4 Formulate a rule for when to add *do* and when to add *does*.

> **Tip**
>
> Statements can be turned into questions by reversing the order of some of the key words or adding *do* or *does* before the verb. Don't forget to add a question mark.
>
> Statement: *You are clever at lessons.* Question: *Are you clever at lessons?*
>
> Statement: *You notice things well.* Question: *Do you notice things well?*

11 Make notes for a storyboard

A Discuss the picture story of *The Lion and the Mouse* with a talk partner.

1 Remind yourself of the different stages of a story.

Introduction	Plot			Ending
	Build-up	Complication /Climax	Resolution	

> **Did you know?**
>
> Fables are short stories, usually with animal characters, that teach a lesson. This fable of the lion and the mouse was first told by Aesop about 2500 years ago! His fables were passed down by word of mouth and were not printed until modern times so there is no 'right' version of the story.

2 With a talk partner, describe what you see happening in each picture, thinking about the different stages in a story.
- Who are the characters and what is the setting?
- What is the problem that needs to be solved?
- How is it solved?

3 Imagine what the characters would say to each other. Make notes.
- What questions do they ask?
- What replies do they give?
- What tone do they use?

4 Choose a proverb that would act as a reflection at the end.
- One good turn deserves another.
- A friend in need is a friend indeed.
- Actions speak louder than words.

Any volunteers?
Why not role play with a friend to help you think of some dialogue?

Tip
A proverb is a memorable saying that teaches an important life lesson.

B Record your reading of the picture story in your reading log. Comment on reading a story with no words!

68 Unit 4 Just imagine

12 Present a storyboard of *The Lion and the Mouse*

A Tell the story using dialogue.

1 Write what each character says in storyboard form, frame by frame.

2 Rehearse your dialogue to ensure it flows and sounds authentic – the way the characters might actually speak.
- Consider setting your role play in a historical setting using old-fashioned words.
- Consider the lion or the mouse having a distinctive accent or coming from far away. What interesting expressions might they use?

Tip

Psst! Don't forget contractions, exclamations and informal expressions are used in conversation. Wha-hay!

3 Make changes to the dialogue if you need to. Consider what descriptive adverbs you might have used if you were writing out the dialogue with narrative: *suspiciously, regretfully, enthusiastically, thoughtfully,* etc.

B Perform a role play of your storyboard for the class, ending with your chosen proverb. Make your role play lively and fun!

Break a leg!

Session 12 Present a storyboard of *The Lion and the Mouse*

5 Making the news

Information is everywhere. We learn about events in the world from the news and we discover what life was like long ago when we visit museums. In this unit, you'll read news articles, look at a museum brochure and put instructions in order. You'll also tell your own news and write a news article.

Vocabulary to learn and use:
inscription, brochure, museum, recent, desert, wilderness, article, summary, report, opinion, skim

1 Share information

A **AZ** What was life like two thousand years ago? It may seem impossible to imagine, but many cultures, like the ancient Egyptians, left clues about how they lived.

70 Unit 5 Making the news

1 Discuss what you think these words mean, using the pictures to help you.

> pyramid   mummy   hieroglyphics   pharaoh   archaeologist   scarab

Tip
Why not make a personal word book? Start with these words!

Did you know?
How the ancient Egyptians built the pyramids is a mystery. Each one probably took 20 to 30 years to complete!

B Use a dictionary to find out more about these words.
1 Put the words into alphabetical order.
2 Use a dictionary to check the meanings of the words.

Tip
When you skim, don't read all the details, just look at the headings, the pictures and the first and last sentence. They'll help you guess the topic.

2 Link it up

A dictionary will tell you the meaning of a word. If you want more information, you have to look elsewhere.

A Archaeologists have discovered objects from thousands of years ago that are keys to the mysteries of ancient worlds.
1 Skim the text to find out what it is about. Then, read it closely.

What is a mummy?
In Ancient Egypt, when important people died, their bodies were preserved or 'mummified' to try to make them last for ever. A preserved ancient body is known as a mummy.

How did they do it?
It took about 70 days to embalm a body. First, all the internal organs were removed. Then, the body was cleansed with palm wine and crushed incense. Next, it was filled with crushed myrrh and other spices. After that, it was covered with a salt mixture which helped to dry it out. Then, the body was wrapped in strips of white linen cloth which had been coated with resin. Finally, the preserved body, or mummy, was placed in a coffin and sealed in a tomb.

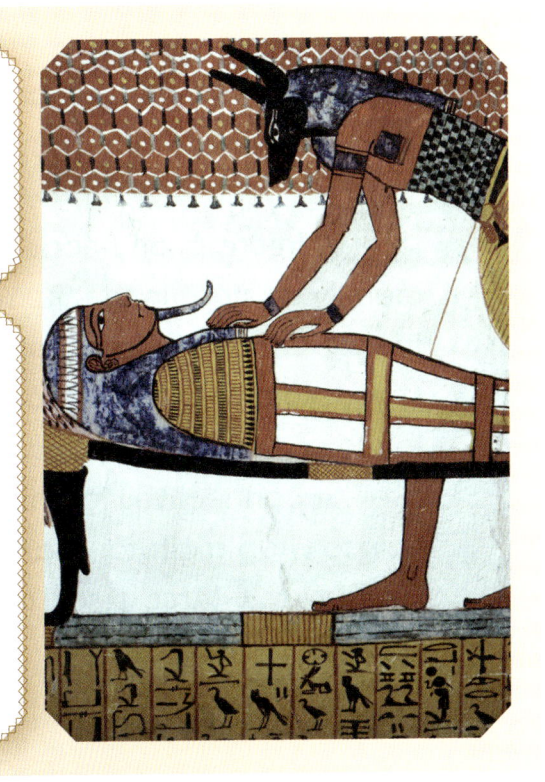

Session 2 Link it up   71

2 Describe the main idea of each paragraph in one sentence. Begin with, *The first paragraph* ...
3 Which tense is the text written in? Why?

Any volunteers?
Who can explain these words?
embalm   preserve

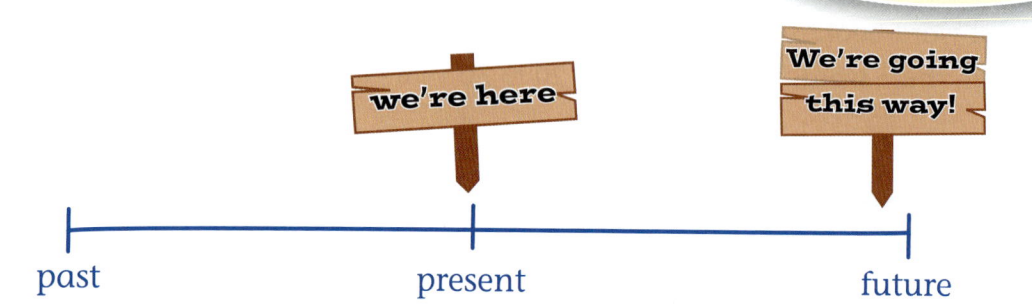

we're here

We're going this way!

past   present   future

Did you know?

The Inca of Peru also made mummies and so did ancient peoples in Australia and on some Pacific islands. Do independent research to find out about some of these ancient civilisations.

B Discuss tenses with your talk partner.
1 What instructions have you had to follow today? Share examples.
2 With a talk partner, take turns to give simple instructions for how to wrap a gift.
3 What tense did you use for the verbs?
4 Now, explain how you wrapped a gift in the past tense!

C Information needs to be in the right order to make sense.
1 Identify six steps in the mummification process. What key words give the sequence of the steps in the process?
2 These words are called **connectives**. They link the sentences and help to make it flow. What punctuation follows after each connective?
3 Use the connectives to write out five or six instructions of your own for how to wrap a gift, for example:
First, cut a large piece of paper.

Unit 5 Making the news

3 Research information

Information and ideas can be presented in many different ways.

A 📖 💬 A model of an ancient man can be seen on display in the Durban Natural Science Museum. Read the **caption** about it.

> **Peten-Amun** was a minor priest in ancient Egypt. He is thought to have died at the age of about 60, a long life by Egyptian standards.

1 What is a caption? What is its purpose?
2 What information is clear from this caption?
3 As a visitor to the museum you might want to know more about the display of Peten-Amun. What questions would you ask?

Have you ever visited a museum? What did you learn about there?

I'd like to ask how they know his name! How can they tell how old he was? What did he look like?

B 📖 Identify the key features of a brochure.
1 Skim part of a museum guide brochure. Describe the layout and the features.
2 What is the brochure about?

Find out about the
AKHMIM MUMMY

Visitors to the museum will be fascinated by the display of ancient Egyptian artefacts, including a model of a man created from a mummy.

Session 3 Research information

The story of Peten-Amun

About 2300 years ago, a man named Peten-Amun (Ptn-'Imn) died in the town of Akhnim in Upper Egypt. Today, a lifelike model of his head and face is on display in the foyer of this museum. According to the hieroglyphics on his coffin, he was probably a minor priest. Scientists believe he was about 60 years old and might have died from old age or an age-related illness.

'Project Mummy'

The reconstruction of the head of Peten-Amun was done in 1990 by Doctor Bill Aulsebrook, a specialist in facial reconstruction. He became fascinated with the challenge of reconstructing the face of someone who lived thousands of years ago! A CAT scan was used to create a three-dimensional model and then Dr Aulsebrook was able to build up the shape of the face around it. The result is a model of what Peten-Amun is thought to have looked like.

Some more words for your word book:
accurate
CAT
reconstruction
three-dimensional

Summarise the information by answering questions.
1. What is the name of the man who was mummified?
2. Who was he?
3. How long ago did he live?
4. Where did he live?
5. For how many years did he live?
6. Who created a lifelike model of his face?
7. When did this take place?
8. Now look carefully at your answers. Which of these answers are facts?

Unit 5 Making the news

9 Which words and phrases in the brochure show that some of the information has been assumed, or is someone's opinion?

10 Write your own short, **factual** summary of the Akhmim Mummy text. Use your answers as facts and make it sound as if there is no doubt about any of the information. Write your summary in 25 to 30 words. For example, change the words *he was probably a priest* to *he was a priest*.

> 'Ducks eat fish' is a fact. 'I *think* ducks *probably* enjoy fish the most' is an opinion!

D Do independent research about another ancient topic. Use key words to make notes. Summarise the information in a brochure to show your friends and family. Remember to use neat, joined-up handwriting when you present your work.

4 Building words

A The English language has grown over hundreds of years. Words have been 'borrowed' from other languages and become part of the language spoken today. **Let's look at some word origins.**

1 Do you know any words used in English that come from other languages?

2 Have a guess where the word *mummy* comes from. Write your idea down, with a made-up reason or story. Share ideas and decide which sounds the most convincing.

3 Now read the explanation of the word's origin on page 76.

> *Aquanaut* comes from two words *aqua* which is Latin for 'water' and *naut* which is Greek for 'sailor'.

Did you know?

The study of where words came from is called **etymology**.

Where does the word 'mummy' come from?

Over the years, the white linen cloth wrapped around mummies went black. This made modern-day scientists think that a black tar mixture called bitumen had been used to preserve the bodies. The Persian word for bitumen is *mummia* and so today we use the term 'mummy'.

Did anyone's guess come close to this?

4 Now, try to tell your talk partner the real explanation in your own words without looking back at the answer.

B Build words from other words with a similar meaning.

Language focus

A word can be changed from one part of speech to another:
e.g. *mummy* (noun), *mummify* (verb) and *mummified* (adjective).
Another way of building words is when a proper noun (the name of a place) is changed to describe something:
e.g. a pyramid in *Egypt* (proper noun) – an *Egyptian* pyramid (proper adjective)

1 Change these nouns into verbs or adjectives with a related meaning.
   a Take turns to use the words in sentences.
   b How many other examples can you think of?

> archaeologist   discoverer
> reconstruction   decision   water

Tip
Need some **help** with this? A dictionary **helps**. It's a **helper**.

2 Change the following proper nouns into proper adjectives to match the object each describes.

Africa	bush
India	elephant
China	food
Italy	clothes
South America	jungle

Tip
A proper adjective must be written with a capital letter.

3 Think of other examples to add to your list.

Unit 5 Making the news

5 Compare information texts

Did you know?
Newspaper articles contain factual information and opinions.

A 💬 **Compare the features of a brochure with those of a newspaper.**

1 Compare a newspaper and a brochure. In two columns, make lists of key features for each.
2 Discuss their differences and similarities.

B 📖 💬 **Use one newspaper per group to find information and details.**

1 Find as many items from this list as possible. Cut them out and make a collage, or label them with sticky labels. See which group can finish first!
- the name and date of the newspaper
- the price of the newspaper
- an example of a headline
- an example of a page number
- sports news and sports results
- the weather forecast
- a schedule or timetable, e.g. a TV or movie guide
- an advertisement
- pictures or photographs
- financial news

Any volunteers? Who'd like to report their group's answers to the class?

2 Design a checklist to identify the features of a newspaper. Use your checklist to compare different newspapers.
3 Did all the newspapers have all the items? Can you explain why? Write a summary of your findings.

How did I do?

- Can I tell the difference between a brochure and a newspaper?
- Can I name some features of each of these texts?
- Can I explain why not all newspapers have exactly the same features?

Session 5 Compare information texts

6 Ask questions

Have you heard the expression, *If you don't ask you won't get* or *You'll only know if you ask?* Questions help you to find answers.

A What can you find out by reading a headline?

Mummy mystery baffles experts

1. Who is mentioned in the headline?
2. Which words are used to make the article sound interesting?
3. What do you think the article is about?

B News articles give important details usually in the first paragraph, telling us the answers to: Who? What? Where? When?

The rest of the article will tell you *how* and *why* the event happened.

Tip
Paragraphs are clear sections in a text that begin on a new line and deal with one main idea.

1. Read the article then make up some questions using these question words. Write the questions and answers in your notebook.
2. With a talk partner, compare your questions. Did each one begin with a question word and end with a question mark?
3. Make corrections if needed and discuss them with the group.

C Does a news article include only the facts in a story? Go through the article again to find out.

1. Use the question words to identify four facts in the article: Who? What? Where? When?
2. Now find opinions – information that comes from someone's ideas or beliefs. Look for the language clues.
3. Explain why a newspaper article might include both facts and opinions.

Language focus

A fact is information that you can be sure of. Opinions are expressed with words like:
maybe   might   could   may   consider
hope   think   feel   believe   understand
imagine   have a theory

And that's a fact!

Unit 5 Making the news

Date ↓
Weekly News June 7 1903

Headline ↓

Mummy mystery baffles experts

By J Robertson ← Reporter's name

Last week, archaeologists working in the **Valley of the Kings** in Egypt announced they had uncovered two mummies. One of the mummies was found in a coffin while the other was lying on the ground. According to archaeologists, the simple tomb indicates that the mummies were not particularly important people, but other clues suggest that they were.

Firstly, the mummies were found in the royal burial area. Secondly, the mummy that was on the ground was placed in the position used to show royalty with the left arm crossed over the chest and the fist clenched. Scientists are puzzled about who it could be. Some believe that she was a servant, while others have a theory that it is the body of Queen Hatshepsut, a powerful pharaoh who ruled about 3500 years ago.

Professor Able, leader of the excavation, says, "We will continue working in the area until we find clues that will help us solve this mystery".

Valley of the Kings a valley where many pharaohs and important nobles were buried

Session 6 Ask questions

7 Ordering information

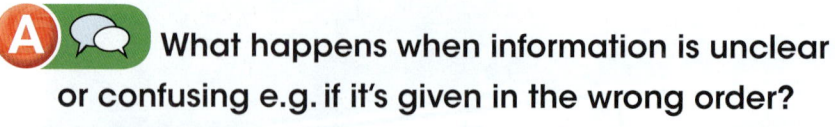

A What happens when information is unclear or confusing e.g. if it's given in the wrong order?

Any volunteers? Who'd like to share some real-life examples?

1 Connectives help to order events. Find these connectives in the mummy mystery text: *last week, while, firstly, secondly, until.*

2 With your talk partner, take turns to tell the story of the mummy mystery, keeping the events in the correct order. Use connectives to help order the events e.g. *to begin with, at first, then, and, so, but, until.*

B Read these details about how the mummy mystery was finally solved.

1 What do you notice about how it is ordered?

How modern science solved the mystery
- Finally, it was concluded that Queen Hatshepsut had been found.
- As a result, the scans revealed that one mummy had a tooth missing.
- Subsequently they found there was an **inscription** on the box in hieroglyphics.
- So, the mouths of both mummies were scanned.
- The 'royal' tooth in the box matched the shape of the gap in the mouth of one of the mummies.
- It all began when a small wooden box was found in a tomb near Queen Hatshepsut's temple.
- According to the **inscription**, the box contained one of Queen Hatshepsut's teeth.

inscription *n.* something that is written or carved on an object

2 What would make this information easier to follow?
3 Draw a simple timeline to work out the order of events. Note key words and phrases to record when the mummy mystery began and when it was finally solved.

Use the connectives in the text as clues to help you order the information.

Unit 5 Making the news

8 Write a headline

A 📖 📝 Newspapers are full of articles with headlines. Why should headlines sound interesting? Let's find out.

1 Read these headlines. Do any sound interesting? Explain why.

> **Scientists are trying to work something out**

> **Nobody knows anything about some old things found recently**

> **Archaeologists have found more old items**

2 Change the language and vocabulary to make them sound more interesting and exciting to the reader. Look through a newspaper and find other headlines that you think sound interesting. Make a poster collage of these headlines.

B 📝 Investigate what headlines do.

1 Write this checklist into your notebook and use it to help you assess your headlines. Decide which ones do a particularly good job.

2 In groups, come up with ideas and write headlines for things that have happened in the past week at school. Use the headline checklist to help make it interesting. Here are some examples:

What headlines do:

	yes	no	comment
Get your attention	–	–	–
Can shock, amuse or inform	–	–	–
Summarise the main idea	–	–	–
Use few words	–	–	–
Use clever language	–	–	–
Make statements, ask questions or use exclamations	–	–	–

> **Omar scores a 6**

> **Honesty wins, lost property returns!**

> **Three cheers for Gabriella**

> **Which team will win?**

3 Now that you can write a good headline, write one for how the mummy mystery was solved after so many years.

Session 8 Write a headline

9 Use varying tenses

A 💬 News is usually told in the past or the present tense. Why do we use the future tense less often to tell news?

1. Take turns telling the whole mummy mystery story without going back to read the text. Tell it in the past tense.

> See who can remember the events and details in the correct order!

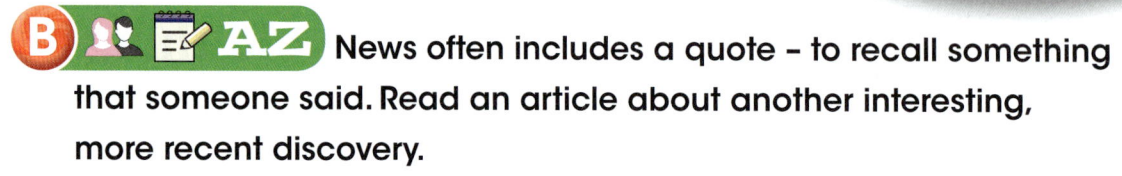

B 👤 📝 AZ News often includes a quote – to recall something that someone said. Read an article about another interesting, more recent discovery.

1. Read the article aloud. You will need two characters to read the direct speech and someone to narrate the rest.

Boy, 3, discovers valuable treasure

A young treasure hunter found a gold pendant worth over £2 million when trying out his dad's metal detector! Three-year-old James was with his dad scanning the earth when, as he put it, "It went beep, beep, beep". His dad said it was beginner's luck. "He got a buzz after just five minutes. It was his first time. I've been doing this as a hobby for 15 years and I've never found anything!" Experts believe the rare piece of jewellery dates back to the 1500s. "James was so excited to find 'treasure' but he has no idea how valuable it is", his dad said. According to James, "We didn't have a map because only pirates have treasure maps".

Tip
The inverted commas show the direct speech.

> I'd like to be the dad! He has the most exciting bits to say!

Unit 5 Making the news

2. Identify the tense of the underlined words in the article.
3. Explain to your partner why some of the dialogue is in the past tense.
4. Rewrite sentences **a** to **d** into your notebook:
   - add inverted commas to show the direct speech
   - change the direct speech to the present tense.

   a. His dad gloated, I was very proud of him.
   b. She exclaimed, We were surprised at its great value.
   c. They were lucky to have found it so quickly, She admitted.
   d. Was it true? She enquired.

How did I do?

- Can I make up an interesting headline?
- Can I recall events in the past tense?
- Can I use the correct form of the verb **to be**?
- Do I know how to include a quote?

Tip

Look out for the verb *to be* and *to have* in these sentences.

10 Keeping things in order

A AZ Imagine going on your own treasure hunt! How would you prepare for a trip to visit the pyramids in Egypt?

1. Describe what you see in the pictures. Make a list of nouns and add adjectives that describe them e.g. *large pyramids*.
2. Discuss what clothes and equipment you might pack.

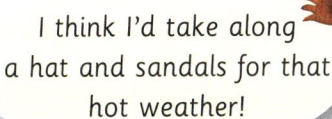

I think I'd take along a hat and sandals for that hot weather!

Session 10 Keeping things in order 83

B The desert is not a good place to be lost! Bear Grylls is a famous adventurer and explorer. His survival tips could save your life.

THE GOLDEN RULE

Bear Grylls

with deserts is never wander off on your own. The priorities of survival are always safety, rescue, water and food. Take cover from the sun. Find a shelter or make one. Stay visible by leaving a sign or clue. Drink sparingly. Eat only if you have water because food makes you thirsty. Conserve your energy, keep calm and don't panic!

1. Read the text. What is its purpose?
2. Give it a title.
3. Are there mainly facts or opinions in the text? Explain why.
4. Identify the instructions. Make a list of the command verbs used.
5. Summarise the text.
    a. Rewrite the text as a list of ten short instructions.
    b. Share and compare your list with a talk partner.

Did you know?
A title is different from a headline. A title says what the text is about without trying to get a reaction from the reader.

Tip
Command verbs leave out the subject.

(You) **Pack** your bags, **grab** your gear and **go**!

Unit 5 Making the news

11 and 12 Write a news article

What news do you have? Most of us have rather ordinary things to tell about.

A Read a news article found on the internet.

1 From the headline and the first two paragraphs, explain what the article is about in one sentence.
2 Make up three questions that you would like to ask about what happened.

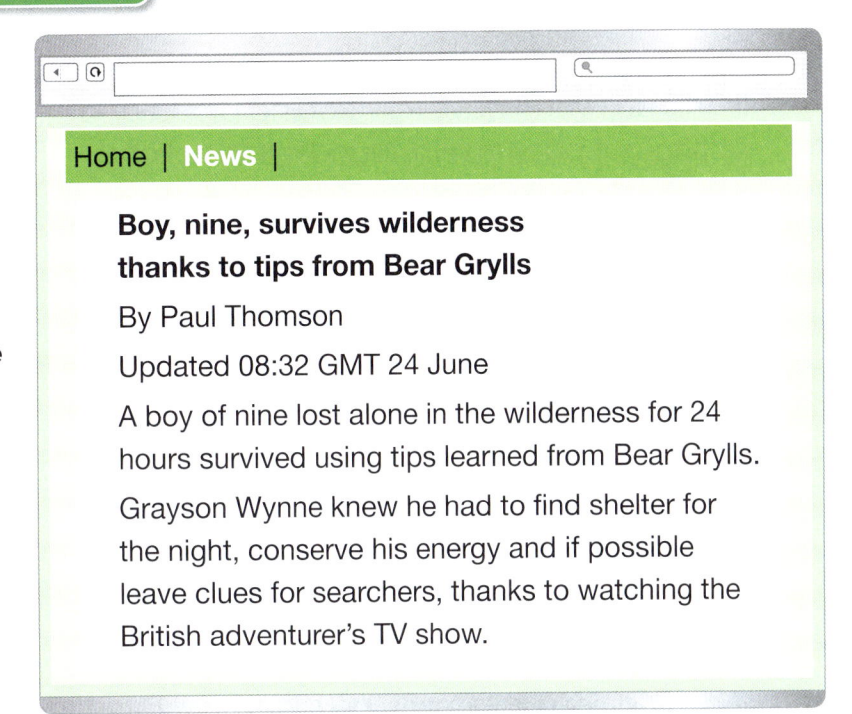

Home | News |

Boy, nine, survives wilderness thanks to tips from Bear Grylls

By Paul Thomson

Updated 08:32 GMT 24 June

A boy of nine lost alone in the wilderness for 24 hours survived using tips learned from Bear Grylls.

Grayson Wynne knew he had to find shelter for the night, conserve his energy and if possible leave clues for searchers, thanks to watching the British adventurer's TV show.

B Have you ever been on an interesting trip, or lost or found something?

1 Tell your news to a talk partner. It can be news about something that happened to you long ago or it could have happened recently.
   - Tell your news in the past tense.
   - Sequence the events in the correct order.
   - Include some facts and some opinion.
   - Speak clearly!
2 Now present your article on paper.
   - Make up an interesting headline for your news.
   - Write out your newspaper article and check it thoroughly.
   - Swap with a partner and check each other's work.
   - Add an invented author name!
   - Write it out again using neat, joined-up handwriting.
3 Set up a class bulletin board. Display your article and read each other's news. Can you guess who wrote what? Have fun trying to work it out!

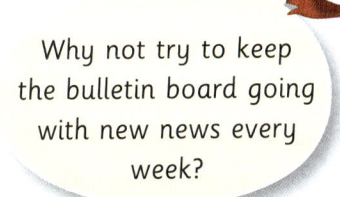

Why not try to keep the bulletin board going with new news every week?

DUCK EGGS START TO HATCH
BABY DUCK ARRIVES
DUCK LEARNS TO SWIM

6 Sensational poems

In this unit you'll have fun reading aloud and acting out poems with sounds and actions. You'll discover how punctuation and shape add expression and meaning to poems. You'll also write your own poems using interesting verbs.

Vocabulary to learn and use:
senses, sounds, image, stanza, expression, pattern, onomatopoeia, assonance

1 Talk about it

A There are sights, sounds and smells all around us.
Our senses help us to connect with the world and make us feel part of it.
1. Close your eyes, be silent and listen to the sounds around you.
2. Discuss all the sounds you heard.
3. Close your eyes again and listen to the poem. Imagine the setting.

Close your eyes, listen and imagine the sights, sounds and smells in the poem.

Did you know?
Mossie (pronounced 'mozzie') is short for *mosquito* – a tiny, flying, biting insect found in warm, damp climates.

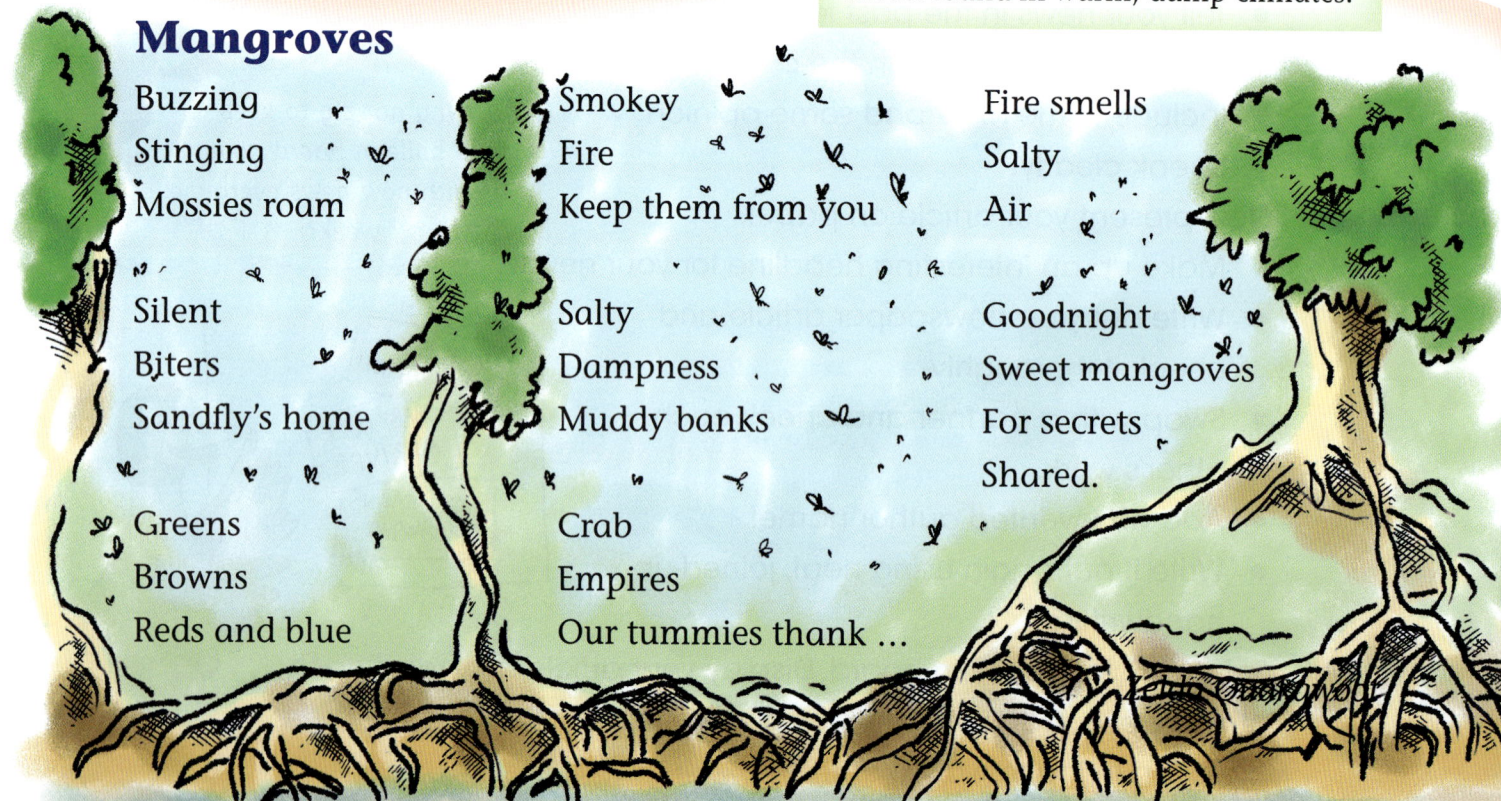

Mangroves

Buzzing
Stinging
Mossies roam

Silent
Biters
Sandfly's home

Greens
Browns
Reds and blue

Smokey
Fire
Keep them from you

Salty
Dampness
Muddy banks

Crab
Empires
Our tummies thank …

Fire smells
Salty
Air

Goodnight
Sweet mangroves
For secrets
Shared.

B 📖 💬 **AZ** Read the poem and discuss the questions.
1. What word is used to describe the sound in the first stanza?
2. What colours can the writer see?
3. What things can the writer feel on her skin?
4. The writer uses the word *salty* twice. What is salty?
5. What can the writer smell?
6. Where do you think the writer is?

2 Hear the sounds

B 📖 **AZ** Read the following poem **silently** before you read it aloud.

The Washing Machine

It goes fwunkety,
then shlunkety,
as the washing goes around

The water spluncheses,
and it shluncheses,
as the washing goes around

As you pick it out it splocheses,
then it flocheses,
as the washing goes around.

But at the end it schlopperies,
and then flopperies,
and the washing stops going round.
　　　　　　　　Jeffrey Davies

Tip
There are many ways to write the **sh** sound:
ma**ch**ine spe**ci**al **s**ugar pen**si**on mi**ssi**on pre**ss**ure na**ti**on

Session 2 Hear the sounds 87

B Now, take turns to read the poem aloud.

1 Read the poem to a talk partner expressively.
2 How was it? Did you prefer to read the poem silently or aloud? Why?
3 Look at all the words that describe a noise. Which words do you think have been made up by the poet? Can you guess their meanings?
4 Why do you think the poet made up these words?

C Use existing words and make up words to describe sounds.

1 Can you think of any other words that describe a sound e.g. toot toot?
2 Think of real words or invent your own to describe the noise made by:
- a fire
- running water
- a crowd of people
- activity on a building site
- a bag of sweets being opened.

Did you know?

When a word sounds like the noise it describes this is called **onomatopoeia**.

Snap!

BOOM!

Ooze …

Whizz!

Any volunteers? Who can say these words with expression?

Unit 6 Sensational poems

D Explore descriptive verbs in a poem.

1 Replace the verbs below with verbs that describe a sound and end in **ing**. The first one has been done for you.
   a man walking → stomping, tramping, marching, plodding
   b plane flying
   c old man sleeping
   d children playing
   e mouse eating

2 Read this poem aloud, with expression.
3 Identify the verbs that show onomatopoeia.
4 What do you notice about the structure of the poem?
5 What is the effect of repeating **ing** at the end of every line?

Dinner Time

Pots bashing!
Water splashing!
Whisk whizzing!
Butter sizzling …

Cutlery banging!
Plates clanging!
Kettle singing!
Oven bell pinging …

Dinner's ready!

Debbie Ridgard

Language focus

Instead of saying
The pots and pans fell onto the floor,
you can use a verb that describes a sound:
*The pots and pans **clattered** onto the floor.*

E Add the poems you've read to your reading log. Make a note of any favourites.

Did you know?

Onomatopoeia comes from the Greek word meaning 'I make'.

3 Rhyming patterns

A Not every poem has to rhyme but many poems do. Rhyme has a purpose. It can create an element of fun, humour or flow and make poems easier to remember.

1 What creates rhyme? Is it the letters and sounds at the beginning, the middle or the end of the words?
2 Read the poems in this unit again and work out their rhyming patterns.

Session 3 Rhyming patterns **89**

B Using onomatopoeia, write your own poem.
1. Choose a topic. Here are some ideas:
   - Getting ready for school
   - Last lesson of the day
   - The plumber fixing a leak
   - A bus ride
2. Make a list of all the sounds that you relate to this topic. Use interesting and descriptive verbs. The verbs should end in **ing**.
3. Write your own sound poem, following the structure of the poem *Dinner Time*. You can choose your own rhyming pattern.
4. Perform your poem! Read it aloud with expression and actions.

Tip
The structure of *Dinner Time* is very simple. It doesn't use any adjectives, just some interesting verbs and sounds.

How did I do?
- Did I use onomatopoeia words?
- Did I work out a rhyming pattern?
- Did I make up my own rhyming pattern?

4 Assonance

A When words have the same vowel sound we call it **assonance**.
1. In the following pairs of words, identify the vowel sounds. Are the vowel sounds made with the same letters?

   see – flea, spoke – croak, play – afraid, tune – balloon

2. Read these words aloud and group the words with the same vowel sound.

   dye fails bee clearing bluesy blowing sight whale donkey
   deer flu floats flies taking quay piers chews poke

3. Work together and come up with other examples of assonance.

Tip
Assonance can create a mood.

Long vowel sounds create a slow pace and a sombre, serious mood.

Short, sharp vowel sounds create high energy and a lighter mood.

Compare the pace and mood of these words:

sorrow
tomorrow
flow
below

light
delight
bright
sight
flight

Unit 6 Sensational poems

5 Punctuation gives expression

A Poets use punctuation, or choose not to use it, to create mood and expression in a poem.

1 Read these words and phrases aloud by following the punctuation, or lack of it.

> Silence **PLEASE!**
>
> Five … Four … Three … Two … One … **GO!**
>
> Here's the big, Bigger, BIGGEST idea!
>
> tick **tock** tick **tock** tick **tock** tick **tock**

2 Then, think of your own examples to add to this list.

B Show your understanding.

1 Listen to the final stanza from the poem, *Foul Shot*. Can you work out what the poem is about?

There's a clue in the title!

The scene: in a game of basketball, the scores are even, a foul is awarded and a player aims and shoots the ball towards the net.

The ball
Slides up and out,
Lands,
Leans,
Wobbles,
Wavers,
Hesitates,
Exasperates,
Plays it coy
Until every face begs with unsounding screams –
And then
                And then
                              And then,
Right before ROAR-UP,
Dives down and through.

Edwin Hoey

2 Read the poem aloud yourself, following the punctuation clues.
3 How does the punctuation affect the way you read the poem?
4 Explain how the comma is used for effect.
5 What phrase is repeated? Explain the purpose of this.
6 Why are some words in capital letters?
7 Describe the mood and how the punctuation is used to create it.

6 Shape poems

A Words and poems can be written in the form of a shape or picture. Read the shape poem opposite and answer the questions.
1 What do you notice about the shape of the poem?
2 What interesting punctuation has the poet used?
3 What effect is created by the repetition of the letter *ppppp* and the words *bubble bubble froth trouble*?
4 Identify the onomatopoeia in the poem.
5 Identify the rhyming words. What is the rhyming pattern?
6 How would you read it aloud?

B Remember to update your reading log with the poems you've read. Which is your favourite now?

C Create a shape poem of your own.
1 Choose a topic from this list and brainstorm verbs and onomatopoeia connected with this topic:
- On a merry-go-round
- Rollercoaster ride
- Awakening volcano
- Questions in my head
- Stormy weather

2 Enjoy using your words to make a picture poem that looks and sounds like the topic. Be as creative as you like!
3 Have fun sharing your poems with each other.

> **Tip**
> Brainstorming is a great way to get all your ideas down quickly. You can make notes from this or add notes to it as you go along. Once all your ideas are recorded, go ahead and write a first draft!

> **Tip**
> Remember to use interesting punctuation.

Unit 6 Sensational poems

Careful When You Pour

Start at the bottom

ppppppppppppppppppppppppppp
pppppppppppppppppppppppp
pppppppppppppppppppp
pppppppppppppppp
pppppppppp
pppppp

right over the topppppp

bubble bubble froth trouble
bubble bubble froth trouble
bubble bubble froth trouble
is it time to stop...?
plink plink hisss hisss
right up to the top
pour me very gently
fizzy whizzy pop
liberate the carbonated
do not spill a drop
gurgle gurgle splish splash

Paul Cookson

Session 6 Shape poems

7 What would you do?

Life is full of surprises and things we have to deal with. These story extracts show us how people deal with the problems and adventures of everyday life. You will also look at 'colourful' English, especially in informal speech and writing.

Vocabulary to learn and use:
formal, informal, slang, jargon, colloquial, idiom

1 Food for thought

A Language can be formal or informal depending on the occasion. **Match each term to its meaning and discuss whether it is formal or informal.**

- jargon
- slang
- colloquial
- idiom

- casual or invented words and expressions
- words and phrases used for particular activities
- a group of words with a meaning that cannot be guessed from the meanings of the separate words
- general conversational language

Unit 7 What would you do?

B 💬 When we speak to friends and family, we often shorten or leave words out. We often use unusual expressions because we know they will understand. This is called speaking colloquial English.

don't be cross with me
eat all my food
relax
nutritious food
you're not in trouble
something to think about

a square meal
you're off the hook
food for thought
eat me out of house and home
chill out!
don't bite my head off

1 Work with a talk partner to match each phrase on the left of the machine with its colloquial partner on the right.
2 The expressions on the right of the machine are called **idioms**. Discuss whether idioms are literal or figurative expressions.

Tip

Remember literal language is the exact meaning of words; figurative language creates mind pictures or images to express meaning.

3 With your talk partner, invent a conversation using some of the idiomatic phrases coming from the machine.

Tip

Using language like this is known as 'adding colour'.
Is 'adding colour' literal or figurative language?

Session 1 Food for thought   95

4 Sometimes we need to use formal language, at other times we can use more informal or colloquial language.
   a Discuss which occasions would require formal or informal language. Give a reason for each to share with the class.
   - a prize-giving speech
   - an interview with the school principal
   - a conversation with a friend in the playground
   - a newscast on the television or radio
   - an email message to a family member
   b Think of other occasions to use informal and formal language.

C Words that are commonly used for a particular activity are often known as **jargon**. People who do that activity are likely to understand these words, but not everyone would. Work in a group to discuss what activity these jargon words belong to.
1 header, dribble, shoot, penalty, pass, corner
2 plain, pearl, needles, yarn, cast on
3 spinner, googly, bails, stumps, slip, runs
4 virus, icon, bit, byte, spyware, jpeg
5 scrum, try, lock, prop, flank, hooker
6 dice, simmer, sieve, beat, whip, knead

D Analyse the language you use with your friends. Come up with a list of words and expressions you often use.
1 Are they idioms or well-known expressions?
2 Would anybody of any age understand them?
3 Do they give another meaning to a regular word? (e.g. *cool*.)
4 Are they related to a particular activity?

2 Making difficult decisions

A 📖 💬 Flying kites is popular the world over, especially in Afghanistan, China and Korea. It can be very technical and kite flyers are very skilled.

1   What term describes these words associated with kite flying?

> reel   sail   frame   bridle   tail   line   wind   pitch   roll   launch   leeward

> "You are driving me mad – just go fly a kite and get out of my hair."

2   The extract below is from *The Kite Fighters* by Linda Sue Park. What do you think *kite fighting* is – a game, a sport or a battle? Why?

3   Skim over the extract and jot down notes about the brothers' **dilemma**. What is the difficult decision they are facing?

What do you think this saying means? "Kites rise highest against the wind, not with it."

dilemma *n.* a situation in which a difficult choice has to be made between two different things you could do

The Kite Fighters

Young-sup and his brother Kee-sup have discovered that coating a kite's line with broken pottery and glue makes it faster at cutting other kites' lines.

As they were busy congratulating each other, Young-sup had a sudden, sobering thought.

"Brother. What if it's against the rules?"

"Against the rules?" Kee-sup stopped in his tracks. "I never thought of that. You mean, maybe someone has thought of this before and it's not allowed."

"We could ask."

"But if we ask another flier, and no one *has* thought of it before, maybe he'll steal our idea."

They stared at each other, their faces reflections of worry.

…

Session 2 Making difficult decisions

"**Honorable** Sir!"

Kite Seller Chung lifted his head. He was just leaving the marketplace after a busy day.

Young-sup rushed up to him, panting from his run, and bowed politely if hurriedly. The old kite seller smiled at his eagerness.

"What demon chases you, young flier?" he teased.

"No demon, sir – just a question."

"A question for me, I take it."

Young-sup looked around them. The market was closing for the day, with many people brushing past them in a hurry to make last-minute purchases. He bowed again to the old man.

"I do not wish to delay you, sir. Perhaps we could talk as I walk beside you."

The old man cocked his head curiously and gestured his **assent**. They set out on the road away from the market and walked in silence until the crowds around them had thinned somewhat.

"Now, young flier. What is this question, the answer to which you believe I hold?"

"It's about the kite festival, sir. About the competition."

"Ah – the kite fights." The old man's eyes lit up with keen interest.

"Yes, sir. It is said that there is little you do not know about them."

The kite seller nodded. "True enough. I have been watching them every year now for more than half a hundred years."

"Then you would know, sir, about the rules." Young-sup paused, his voice low and urgent. "My brother has a new … invention. We wish to use it at the fights, but we need to know if using it would be honorable – within the rules."

His companion frowned. "That is not one question, young flier, but two. Tell me about this invention."

Linda Sue Park

---

honorable *a.* American spelling of *honourable*
assent *n.* agreement or approval

B 📖 💬 **Think about the story structure.**

1 Where in the story do you think this dilemma occurs – towards the start, the middle or the end? Give a reason based on your knowledge of story structure.
2 The extract is from Chapter 11 of 16 chapters – does this support your previous answer? Why?
3 Chapters are mini stories within the bigger story. What do you think the next chapter will be about?

3 Summarise your understanding

A 💬 **With a talk partner, discuss answers to these questions.**

1 Why were the brothers congratulating each other?
2 Do you think Kee-sup or Young-sup is older? Why?
3 What do they think could be *against the rules*?
4 Why don't they just ask another kite flier?
5 Who does Young-sup ask in the end?
6 What two things does Young-sup want to know?
7 Do you think Young-sup's choice of person to ask is a good one? Why?
8 Did the boys do the right thing by asking about their new technique?
9 What answer do you think Young-sup will receive? Why?
10 What answer would you give to Young-sup?

B 📝 **The kite seller's parting words make the boys' decision even harder.**

"But there is a more difficult question. From what you have told me, it is clearly a great advantage – perhaps too great. Yet you say that there would be no advantage without skill. It is you yourself, and your brother, who must decide if it is honorable."

1 Write two paragraphs on the extract and the kite seller's parting words.
- Paragraph 1: summarise the extract's main points. Start with:
  The boys realise their invention might be against competition rules so Young-sup asks ...
- Paragraph 2: explain the dilemma and what you think the boys should do.
  The boys think that ... I think they should ... because ...

Session 3 Summarise your understanding

2 Exchange paragraphs with your talk partner to check for flow and sense.

Any volunteers? Who'd like to share their paragraph with the class?

Tip
- Give the facts before giving your opinion.
- Paragraphs can separate different types of information or introduce a new idea, action, place or speaker.

C Update your reading log and note what you thought of *The Kite Fighters* extract.

Did you know?
The Kite Fighters is set in Seoul, Korea, in 1473, when kite fighting competitions really took place.

4 Focus on the language

A This story is a historical novel.
1 What clue in the boys' conversation suggests that the setting is not modern?
2 Find examples of informal language in the dialogue.
3 **a** Which adjectives describe Young-sup's behaviour towards the kite seller?

> casual   polite   careless   formal   respectful   nervous   excited

  b Why do you think he behaves this way?
  c What does it tell you about Young-sup's character?
  d Do you think he would speak differently in a novel with a modern setting? Why?

4 **a** Which synonyms for *fight* fit the context of kite fights?

> brawl   contest   battle   struggle   skirmish   dispute
> conflict   competition   bout   scrap   match

  b Use three other *fight* synonyms in sentences to demonstrate their meaning.

Tip
Use a dictionary or online vocabulary tool to help you.

B Learn how to use the apostrophe to show possession for plural nouns.
1 Are these possessive form nouns singular or plural?
  a The boys' dilemma. The boy's kites.
  b The parent's complaints. The parents' representative.

Unit 7 What would you do?

Language focus

To show possession of a plural noun:
- Add the apostrophe to the end of the plural noun.
- Does the plural noun already end in **s**?

the brothers' kites

the people's choice

the market sellers' stalls

the children's toys

If not, add an **s** after the apostrophe:
children → children's
people → people's

If so, **don't** add another **s**:
brothers → brothers'
girls → girls'

2 How would you show possession using an apostrophe in these sentences? Write the answers in your notebook.
   a The enamel of the teeth was very white.
   b The wheels of the cars were spinning fast.
   c The work in the first three days was easy.
   d The tails of the losing five kites came off in the wind.

5 Work with sentences

A Practise working with sentences. Write the answers in your notebook.

1 Turn each group of words into a correct sentence.
   a Kee-sup's brother Young-sup.
   b did you ask the kite seller
   c Two questions not one.
   d With many people brushing past.

2 Re-order these words to make sensible sentences.
   a The kite flew Young-sup high in the air.
   b The day was closing for the market.
   c My invention has a new brother for the competition.
   d The old eyes' man lit up with keen interest.

Language focus

- Sentences begin with a capital letter and end with full stop, a question mark, or an exclamation mark.
- Sentences must contain a verb.
- Sentences must make sense.

Tip

Connectives can **join** two sentences or **extend** a sentence. Conjunctions and adverbs often act as connectives.

Session 5 Work with sentences 101

3 Use the context to choose the best connective to join these sentences.
   a The boys were worried. Young-sup consulted the kite seller. (*and, so*)
   b The invention is very clever. It might cause trouble. (*and, but*)
   c We break the rules. We will be disqualified. (*if, and*)
   d Young-sup flew the kite. Kee-sup was the older brother. (*although, because*)
   e I feel the wind speaking to me. I fly the kite. (*but, when*)
   f The boys entered the dragon kite. The king asked them to fly it. (*if, because*)
   g I wanted to make kites. I want to fly kites. (*since, more than*)
   h Please help me. I can make a good kite. (*and, so*)

6 What would you do?

A This extract comes from a story set in Spain. Abuelo, the narrator, and his grandson Antonito are close and talk to each other about many things.

1 Read the extract with a talk partner. Use evidence from the text and your own experience to decide which of these actions made Antonito's mother most cross:
   - He broke the window with a soccer ball.
   - He denied breaking the window.
   - He refused to explain how the window broke.

Any volunteers? Who can guess what *Abuelo* means?

Did you know?

- *Siesta* is a Spanish word meaning a nap in the early afternoon when it is too hot to work. The word has become part of the English language.
- *Toro* means 'bull' in Spanish; it originated from the Latin word *taurus*.

2 What evidence shows that Antonito's grandfather (Abuelo) wasn't cross about Antonito breaking the window? Why do you think Abuelo wasn't cross?

Toro! Toro!

It was a little enough thing that began it. It happened during the siesta. Antonito was bored. He was just messing around, as children do. All he did
5 was kick a football through a window, by accident. When his mother came storming out into the garden, Antonito was standing there in his Barcelona shirt, looking as guilty as sin. He hadn't run off – he's not like that. There
10 was no one else around except the cat and me, and we were having our afternoon nap under the mimosa tree at the bottom of the garden, well away from the scene of the crime. So, Antonito had to be the **culprit**. He was for it, and there was nothing I could do to help him.

"Antonito! How many times have I told you?" I could see that chin of his was
15 jutting already and I knew there'd be tears welling up inside him. I could sense what he was going to say before he even said it. "I didn't do it. It wasn't me. Honest." And it was all said with such utter conviction, such determined defiance. Asked for an alternative explanation, he shrugged insolently at his mother, pursed his lips and refused to speak.

20 *Antonito is banished to his bedroom as punishment. Later, when his grandfather, Abuelo, talks to him about what he saw happen, Antonito asks him some difficult questions.*

"Abuelo, when you were little, did you ever do bad things? I mean, really bad. Did you ever tell a lie?"

25 "Abuelo, when you were little, what was the very worstest thing you ever did?"

Michael Morpurgo

culprit *n.* someone who has done something wrong or is responsible for a bad situation

Session 6 What would you do? 103

B Describe a situation where it was hard for someone to tell the truth.
- Listen carefully to each person's story.
- Discuss why the situation was difficult.
- Comment on each other's stories, allowing each person time to talk.

7 Notice the language

Tip
The question and exclamation marks show you what expression to add.

A The first paragraph is made up of both short and long sentences.

Read the extract aloud, with a talk partner, using the punctuation and different sentence lengths to add expression. Give each other feedback.

Language focus

Groups of words or phrases can act as adjectives or adverbs. The underlined words describe the verb, so they act as an adverb: *He was just messing around with his friends*.

B Adverbs describe **when**, **where** or **how** an action took place.
1 The underlined phrases below are acting as adverbs. Do they describe **when**, **where** or **how** an action happened?
   a He kicked a football through a window <u>by accident</u>.
   b I was having a nap <u>under the tree</u> <u>at the bottom of the garden</u>.
   c <u>Later that evening</u>, Abuelo spoke to Antonito.
2 Add an adverbial phrase to complete these sentences.
   a Antonito kicked the soccer ball (*where*).
   b Abuelo admitted he had also told a lie (*when*).
   c Antonito listened to his grandfather (*how*).
3 Antonito asks his grandfather two questions.
   a Identify the question words used in each.
   b Predict how his grandfather might have answered.

Unit 7 What would you do?

8 Degrees of comparison

Language focus

We can compare nouns using comparative adjectives with the suffixes **er** and **est**.

Adjective	Comparative er	Superlative est
light	lighter	lightest
sad	sadder	saddest
happy	happier	happiest

- Comparative adjectives compare two nouns.
  Antonito is younger than Abuelo.
- Superlative adjectives compare more than two nouns.
  Antonito is the youngest person in the family.

Spell check

mad, ma**dd**er, ma**dd**est   late, lat**e**r, lat**e**st   fit, fit**t**er fit**t**est

happy, happ**i**er, happ**i**est   big, big**g**er, big**g**est

A Work with a talk partner.

1 Choose a ball and write down the related adjectives that would be in the other two balls.

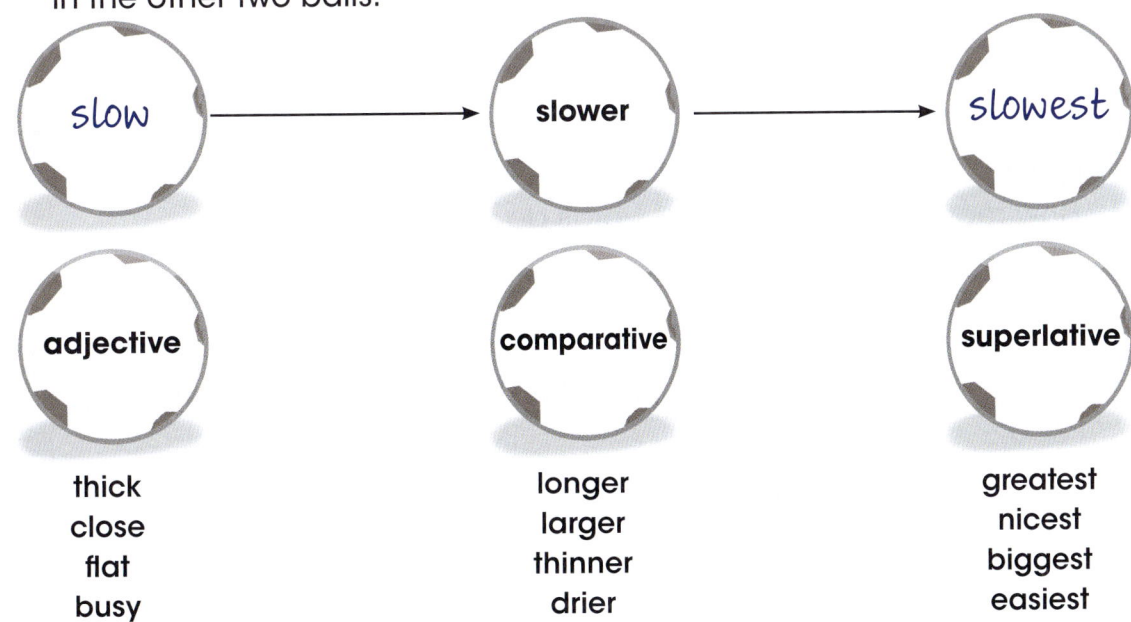

slow → slower → slowest

adjective | comparative | superlative

thick	longer	greatest
close	larger	nicest
flat	thinner	biggest
busy	drier	easiest

2 Use the **Spell check** box to check your spellings.
3 Formulate a rule for each example demonstrated in the spell check.
4 Join two other pairs who worked with different ball sets and compare your answers.

B Choose the correct comparative or superlative adjective to complete these sentences.
1 Antonito was the (*fast*) runner in his class.
2 Antonito's grandfather was usually (*calm*) than his mother.
3 That kick was the (*long*) you have ever kicked!
4 Luckily he broke the (*small*) window in the house.
5 Abuelo is (*kind*) to his grandson than to anyone else.

C Some adjectives use *more* or *most* to form comparatives, especially adjectives with more than two syllables or ones that end in the suffix **ful**: comfortable, more comfortable, most comfortable; painful, more painful, most painful.
1 Choose an adjective from each box and write sentences about Abuelo and Antonito using the comparative and superlative forms.
2 Share your sentences with another pair.

thoughtful   careful   cheerful   hopeful

generous   important   difficult   expensive

D Some verbs have irregular comparative forms.
1 How many of these irregular words do you already know? Discuss examples of when you would use them.

Adjective	Comparative	Superlative
good	better	best
bad	worse	worst
many	more	most
little	less	least

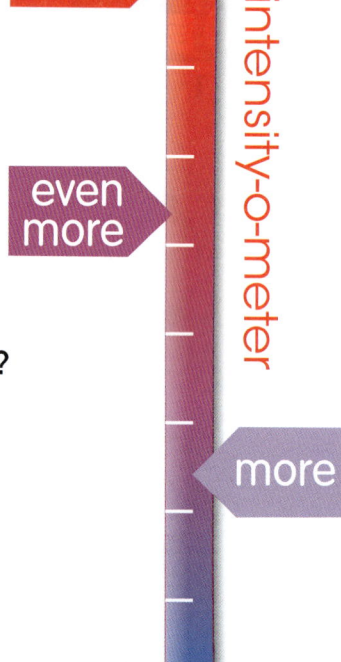

most
even more
more
a bit

intensity-o-meter

Unit 7 What would you do?

2 Choose the correct comparatives to complete this paragraph.

Antonito was (*good*) at football than any other sport. He was (*little*) keen on cricket, and swimming was definitely his (*bad*) sport. (*Many*) than anything, he wanted to be the (*good*) professional soccer player ever.

E Remember to note the *Toro! Toro!* extract in your reading log, with a comment about your reaction to it.

Any volunteers?
Who can find and put right the comparative adjective that Antonito forms incorrectly in the extract?

9 Michael Morpurgo's novel *Cool!*

A In the extract from Michael Morpurgo's novel *Cool!* (on page 108), a local newspaper article explains what has happened to Robbie Ainsley.
1 Use the newspaper article to build up a character profile of Robbie.
   a Based on the news article, come up with a list of adjectives to describe Robbie.
   b Use the adjectives to create an imaginative character profile.
   c Illustrate the profile with pictures you think Robbie would like to see when he wakes up.

B Find out more about being in a coma. Work in groups.
1 Read these answers from Professor Knowalot as well as the ones on page 108 and decide what questions were asked.
   a A serious injury to the head, hurting the brain, can cause a coma.
   b Usually, a coma lasts a few weeks, but it can last for years.
   c Some patients in a coma breathe by themselves; others need machines to help them breathe.
   d Comas can cause unusual things. In 2010, a 13-year-old girl in Croatia came out of her coma speaking German fluently but had forgotten her own language.

Did you know?
The word *coma* comes from the ancient Greek word *koma* meaning 'deep sleep'.

Session 9 *Cool!*

Prayers at school for coma boy

Prayers were said this morning at the primary school in Tiverton for Robbie Ainsley who was knocked down by a car last week. Head teacher Mrs Tinsley said, "Robbie is a very popular boy at school with children and teachers alike. He plays centre forward in the school football team, sings in the choir, and only recently played Oliver Twist in our school production of *Oliver*."

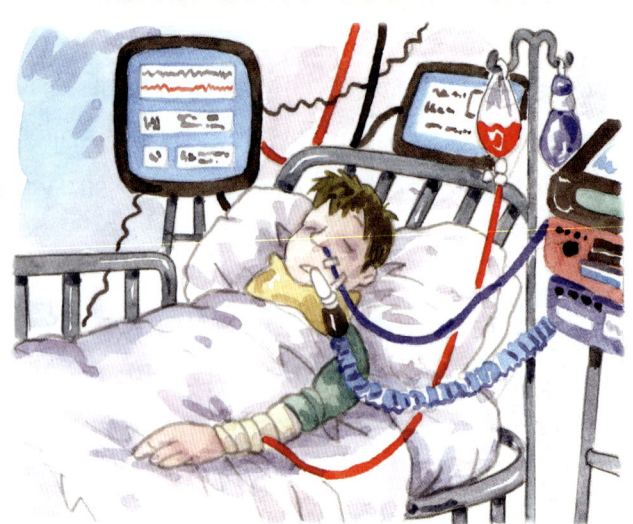

Robbie Ainsley remains in a coma and on a life support system in Wonford Hospital where doctors say his condition is unchanged.

Michael Morpurgo

Did you know?

Michael Morpurgo has written more than 100 books. In 2003 he was made Children's Laureate in the UK, which is an award for outstanding achievements in children's literature.

Fact file

Ask Professor Knowalot

Q: What is a coma?
A: A coma is when a person has been unconscious for more than six hours.
Q: Can people in a coma hear?
A: No-one can be sure. After recovering, some patients recall hearing but not being able to respond.

10 Read about Robbie's classmates

A Robbie's teacher has brought recorded messages from his classmates to cheer him up in hospital.

1 Read the extract closely and write notes on the following:
   a Who is telling the story?
   b Explain how this happens.
   c What does this tell you about Robbie in his coma?
2 Compare your notes with a talk partner.

Robbie hears Marty first

"Hi, Rob. We played St Jude's on Saturday, and we won, of course. We hammered them 4–1. The goal they got was a penalty, which wasn't fair – I never touched their centre forward. He dived. Get better soon because
5 we miss having you around. And we need you back in the team, too. See ya."

"Hiya Robbie. It's Lauren. I'm the new girl who sits in the back and has coloured braids in her hair. You are to get better soon, because we all
10 get very sad when we think of you in hospital. Bye for now."

"Robbie, it's your *Check*mate, Morris." Morris, a real boffin, the school chess champion – looks like Harry Potter – brain like a computer. I only ever beat him
15 once, and then I cheated. Bit of a weirdo. He's always making jokes, and then explaining them as if you're stupid or something. He's doing it now. "*Check*mate. *Check*mate. Get it? *Check*mate. Come back soon, so's I can *check*mate you again. Right?"

Session 10 Read about Robbie's classmates 109

20 "Hey Robbie. This is Barry. Remember me?" Not likely to forget you, am I? Barry being friendly? Barry being nice? "Listen, I just want to say get better, that's all. When you come
25 back we could be mates, yeah?" And he sounds as if he really means it, too. Maybe he's not as bad as I thought after all.

"This is Freya. Can you hear me, Robbie?" That is Freya Porter, who is very quiet and
30 always wears those mules – sort of clog-type shoes. I think her mother's Dutch. She speaks with a bit of an accent, but she's better at spelling than any of us.

"Imran here, Robbie." Bill Sykes in Oliver
35 Twist. "You've got to open your eyes and do stuff, because if you don't, you won't get to be in our next show. I just came back from my holiday in Spain when I heard about your accident, and my mum and my dad and me
40 hope you get better very soon."

Then Sam. Then Juliet. Then Joe. All of them. Everyone in my class. I just want to jump out of this bed, run down the road, across the playground, into the classroom and shout out:
45 "Here I am! I'm back! I'm better!" But all I can do is lie here and cry inside.

Michael Morpurgo

B Read the text as a writer. Work with a talk partner and be ready to share your ideas.

1 How many people speak in the extract?
2 Identify examples of informal language. Explain how they bring the text to life.
3 What tense is this narrative mainly written in?
4 What effect is the writer trying to create by using this tense?
5 What can you work out about Robbie's relationship with Barry before the accident? How does Robbie's view of Barry change?
6 Draw up a mini character profile of one of Robbie's schoolmates.

11 Explore how play scripts work

A When books are turned into plays or films, the story is told through the dialogue and actions of the characters. Play scripts show when each character speaks and what they say. No speech marks are used.

Mrs Tinsley: Now, Robbie. Here's Marty with the first message.
Marty: Hi, Rob. We played St Jude's on Saturday.

1 Write out the conversation below as a play script and discuss a rule for setting out dialogue.

Tip
Only include the character names and the words they actually say in your play script.

"I hope hearing his classmates has cheered him up," sighed Dad.
"I'm sure it has," reassured Tracey, Robbie's nurse, in a cheery voice.
"Robbie will be pleased that his friends are thinking of him."
"And he'll certainly be relieved that his team beat St Jude's!" laughed Dad.

2 Discuss how a play script could tell actors how to act and speak.

Session 11 Explore how play scripts work 111

B 　　　　Develop the play script.

1 Work in groups of eight.
   a Identify the words Robbie says in his head. Change the wording if you need to.
   b Write out each character's words from the extract in dialogue format, including the words Robbie speaks.

Tip

Remember to use neat, joined-up writing so that group members will be easily able to read their parts in the play.

2 Discuss how the part of Robbie could be performed on stage. Imagine the stage scene with friends gathered round Robbie's hospital bed rather than being on tape. Add helpful stage directions to your script.

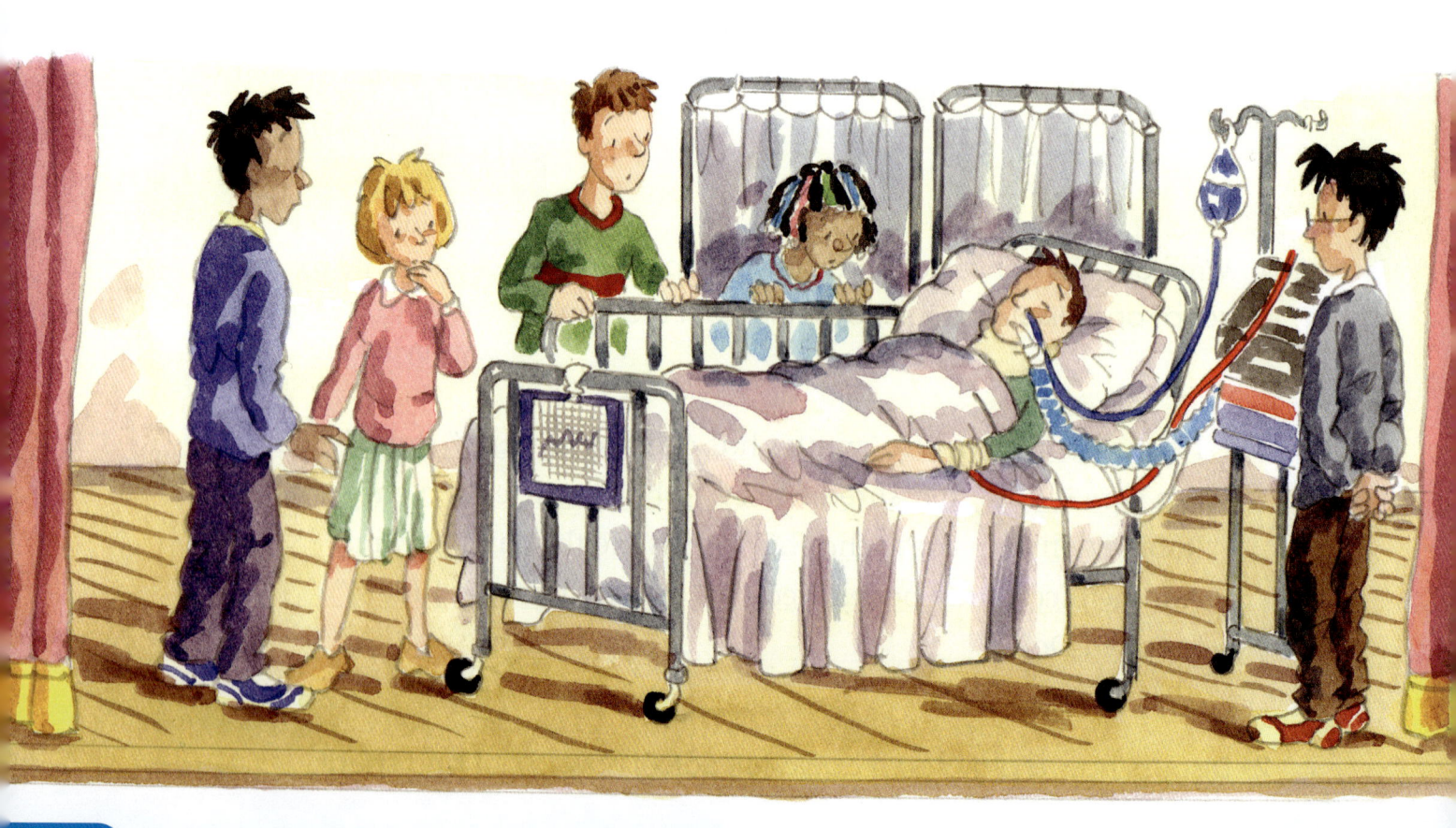

Unit 7 What would you do?

C How did you like this story extract compared with the other Michael Morpurgo extract you read? Make a note in your reading log.

How did I do?

- Have we found a way for Robbie to 'speak' although the others can't hear him?
- Have we got ideas for expression, actions and props to bring the play to life?
- What will we do differently for the final performance?

12 Perform a play script

A Work in groups. Rehearse and perform your play script.

1 Each person acts one role: Robbie, Marty, Lauren, Morris, Barry, Freya, Imran. Practise your play script using expression, actions and props to bring it to life.

2 When you're ready, perform your plays for each other. Have fun seeing what you've all achieved!

Session 12 Perform a play script

8 Food for thought

Food is a big part of our lives. We need it, we spend a lot of time thinking about it and we enjoy sharing the experience of eating it, with family and friends.

In this unit you will hear about some delicious meals, you will follow a recipe, prepare to enter a cooking competition and learn how to promote yourself. You will also analyse an advertisement and a review and learn to use descriptive and persuasive language effectively.

Vocabulary to learn and use:
persuasion, persuasive, emphasise, convincing, dessert, yoghurt, flavoured, advertisement

1 Introducing persuasive language

A Trying a new food can be challenging, especially if it is something you are not used to. You may need a lot of **persuasion**.

1 Skim the text (on the next page). What type of text is it?
2 Practise reading it with expression.
- Which words can you emphasise?
- Where can you add expression and volume?
- How loud will it be?
- Can you use actions or facial expression?

Any volunteers? Who can make it sound like a radio or TV commercial?

B Identify the key features and purpose of the text.
1 Give an example of each of these features from the text.
   a Headings
   b Factual information
   c Visual clues
   d Persuasive language

Freezo-licious

Freezo-licious is a delicious, new frozen yoghurt which is 99% fat free!

Irresistible flavours include classic favourites like chocolate, strawberry and vanilla or more unusual taste sensations like chai tea, pomegranate, kiwi, watermelon or toffee. For healthy toppings, add some fresh fruit and nuts or for those with a sweet tooth try our dessert toppings of shortbread, chocolate sprinkles, caramel bites or marshmallows! To top it off we have a range of yummy sauces including healthy honey, decadent dark chocolate or blissful berry. Why not treat yourself and have one today?

2 Is there a message? Who is the *target market*?
3 What is the purpose of this text?

I don't think it's aimed at me – I don't see any fishy flavours or scaly sprinkles!

C Persuade your friends to try something new.

1 Tell your group about your favourite food, snack or meal. Be *convincing* and persuasive about it. Make your classmates feel eager to try it.

D Record the advertisement in your reading log. What did you think of it?

Session 1 Introducing persuasive language

2 Be descriptive

A Identify and discuss adjectives.

1 Identify the adjectives in the *Freezo-licious* text.
2 Sort the following adjectives into four lists of words with similar meanings:

tempting healthy inviting nutritious new LATEST tasty wholesome delicious irresistible fresh mouth-watering

> **Language focus**
>
> Adjectives describe nouns – objects and feelings. Adjectives are often used for effect.
>
> **This is a <u>nice</u> flavour.**
>
> could become
>
> **This is a <u>scrumptious</u> flavour.**

3 Rewrite these sentences, adding an adjective from your lists to each one:
  a She ate the dessert eagerly.
  b They all chose fruit toppings.
  c Everyone enjoyed the flavours.

4 Write these adjectives as degrees of comparison in sentences.
  a scrumptious
  b tempting
  c delightful
  d healthy
  e tasty

> **Language focus**
>
> When we compare things we use adjectives of comparison.
> *More* is used to compare <u>two things</u> while *the most* compares <u>several things</u>.
> If the word ends in **ful** or has more than two syllables, then it stays the same and you add *more* or *most*. e.g.
> *delicious > more delicious > most delicious*
> *careful > more careful > most careful*
> If the word ends with **y**, the **y** changes to **i** before adding **er** or **est**. e.g.
> *happy > happier > happiest*

B Practise using commas in a list.

1 What do the commas do in this sentence?
   The flavours I like are caramel, kiwi, chocolate and vanilla.
2 Find another example of a list with commas in the *Freezo-licious* text.
3 Write a sentence with a list of your own favourite foods.

4 If you remove the commas, how does the meaning change?
5 Add commas to change the meaning of these sentences:
   a Please will you buy chilli sauce chips and noodles.
   b I love to eat fish cakes, chicken soup and fried onions.

'I like fish, corn and water' **not** 'I like fish corn and water!'

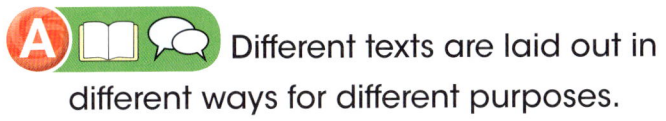

3 Compare layout, purpose, language

A Different texts are laid out in different ways for different purposes.
1 What is the name for this type of text?
2 What do you notice about the layout? Describe some of the features.
3 How is the layout different from the *Freezo-licious* text?
4 Do both texts include facts and opinions? Give some examples.
5 Compare the purpose of these texts. What does each one aim to do?

B Compare the use of language in the two texts.
1 Compare the adjectives in the *Freezo-licious* text with the ones used in the recipe. Which text uses adjectives to show an opinion, and which one uses adjectives to give factual information?

Yoghurt ice cream

Makes about 1.5 litres

You need:
500ml flavoured yoghurt (any flavour)
250ml cream
397g tin condensed milk

Method:
1 Mix yoghurt and condensed milk together until well combined.
2 Beat the cream until stiff and fold into the mixture.
3 Pour the mixture into a plastic container and freeze for five to six hours until set.
4 Serve with a topping of your choice.

Freezo-licious	Recipe
Delicious frozen yoghurt	Flavoured yoghurt
Healthy toppings	Condensed milk
Yummy sauces	Plastic container

2 Compare the following sentences.

> - Freezo-licious is a delicious, new frozen yoghurt which is 99% fat free!
> - Beat the cream until stiff and fold into the mixture.

a Identify the adjectives in each sentence.
b What do you notice about the use of adjectives in each one?
c Rewrite the first sentence as a fact.

Tip
Here's a hint: remove some of the adjectives.

C Instructions are ordered, often numbered and usually begin with a **command verb**
Example: *Beat the cream …*

1 Identify the command verb in each numbered instruction in the recipe on page 117.
2 Write a set of five instructions on how to make a sandwich. Number each instruction and begin each sentence with one of these command verbs.

Cut Spread Add Put Slice Serve

Tip
Remember – you don't need persuasive language when you write instructions.

How did I do?

- Did I use commas correctly in my lists?
- Did I identify when adjectives are being used persuasively?
- Did I write a set of instructions using the command verb?

D Add the recipe to your reading log and write a comment.

Unit 8 Food for thought

4 Analyse an advertisement

A Identify the layout, purpose and language of this text.
1. What sort of text is this? Scan it quickly to decide.
2. What are the key features of this text?
3. Identify the adjectives used to describe these nouns:
   chef, recipe, dish, cook, profile
4. Are the adjectives used to add information, or to persuade the reader, or both?

Super Chef Competition
Calling all keen cooks to the kitchen!

Simply complete the entry form and send it along WITH your favourite recipe AND a personal profile telling us all about yourself and how much you love to cook.

Rules:
1. You must be aged between 9 and 12.
2. All entry forms must be completed and handed in by 1st May.

How it works:
1. Our judges will choose 20 top entrants from all the entries.
2. The top entrants will be interviewed by our panel of expert chefs.
3. Five finalists will have to cook and present their favourite dish AND follow one other mystery recipe.

Prizes:
The top entrants will receive a set of baking utensils.
All finalists will receive a fun, interactive cook book.
The winner will receive a 'dream birthday party' for 50 people!

Session 4 Analyse an advertisement

B 📖 💬 **Identify ways to attract attention.**
1. Discuss how adverts get your attention.
2. Find three different types of sentences in the advertisement.
3. How do they make the text interesting and attractive?
4. Connectives can be used to emphasise a point. Identify the connectives and read each sentence aloud using expression. Then, come up with your own.
   - Buy one AND get one free!
   - It's a sale BUT wait – there's more!
   - You deserve it BECAUSE you're special!
   - You can win a prize IF you enter today.
   - Get a discount WHEN you buy five items.
   - SINCE it's our birthday, we're spoiling you!
   - You've heard about it NOW get it!

> **Attention-grabbers**
> - Bold headings
> - Bright colours
> - Interesting fonts
> - Catchy phrases
> - Questions and exclamations
> - Emphasising connectives
> - Symbols and/or characters
> - Prizes

C 💬 📝 **Answer these questions to see how well you understand the text.**
1. Who is the competition for?
2. How do you enter the competition?
3. What will the finalists have to do?
4. How will they select a winner?
5. What prize do the top entrants receive?

How did I do?
- Did I identify the key features of an advertisement?
- Do I understand how an advertisement gets the reader's attention?

D 📝 **AZ** Record the competition text in your reading log and write a comment.

Language focus
Some instructions have exclamation marks to show how serious, important or exciting the instruction is.

JOIN NOW!   **KEEP OUT!**

Beware!!!! – using too many exclamation marks can look angry!

120   Unit 8 Food for thought

5 Design an advertisement

A 📝 Think of an event you would like to get your friends to attend and design an advert that will persuade them to be there!

1. Decide on your event. You can choose one of these or think of your own.
   - To buy something from your stall on market day
   - To join the Book Day Readathon
   - To be a part of your team for the school fun sports day
   - To attend your birthday party
2. Brainstorm your ideas. Use key words to make notes, then write a first draft.
3. Use the *Attention-grabbers* checklist to plan and design your advert.
4. Be persuasive – make it sound appealing!
5. Check and edit your work before you present it.

6 Introduce yourself

A 💬 Imagine entering a competition like the one in the advertisement. An entry form needs specific details about the person entering.

1. Use this example to tell your talk partner details about yourself.
2. When you and your talk partner have told each other your details, try to remember and repeat back as many facts as you can.

Tip

Take turns. Give only the details required. Listen carefully!

Super Chef Competition Entry Form

Print neatly with a black pen.

Personal details

Full name: Edgar Flores

Age: *(Tick the correct box)*
9 ☐ 10 ☑ 11 ☐ 12 ☐

School: Panay Primary

Extra information

Your favourite healthy meal to make:
oysters and rice

Your favourite dessert to make:
pancakes

Other hobbies and interests
Playing soccer, reading, fishing, being a Boy Scout

Session 6 Introduce yourself 121

B A form is used to gather details about someone for a purpose.
1. Design a form to give to a class member to get to know them better.
   - Ask about basic details first.
   - Then decide on other questions that will help you get to know the person e.g. ask about their hobbies and interests.
   - Keep it simple – have no more than ten questions.
   - Set it out neatly with enough space for the answers.
2. Swap forms with a partner and fill it in.

> **Don't be too personal.**
> You shouldn't ask anything that you wouldn't be happy to answer yourself!

> **Any volunteers?**
> Who can tell the class something interesting they found out about their partner?

7 Write a personal profile

A A profile gives personal details and aims to show the person in 'a good light'.

1. This introduction is written by the author of a cook book. In the introduction, he tells the reader all about himself.
   a. How old do you think Josh is?
   b. How would you describe the language he uses; *friendly, serious, informative, negative, factual, relaxed, positive, persuasive?*
   c. What personal details does Josh include?
   d. How does Josh promote himself and his book? Identify positive words and phrases.

> I love to eat and I love to cook! So I've chosen my favourite 48 recipes of the yummiest food and drinks, which I know you're going to want to make as well. And they're healthy too so your mom will be happy, and so will the rest of your family be when they see what you've made for them. And if you want to play in between, there are fun games too, such as crosswords, connect-the-dots and spot-the-difference.
>
> After I watched the TV shows *MasterChef* and *Junior MasterChef*, I just knew I had to write my own cookbook. I really hope that you will have fun cooking from these recipes! When I'm not cooking, I like to draw, play sport, read and sing.
>
> *Josh*

Unit 8 Food for thought

2 How would you change these sentences to sound more persuasive:
   a I enjoy cooking food.
   b I'd like to enter this competition.
   c I am a good cook.
   d You'll like my recipes and ideas.

> **Tip**
> Use strong verbs and add interesting adjectives!
> I can make nice cakes.
> I can bake delicious cakes.

B Practise being persuasive.

1 Write your own personal profile. Choose one of the following topics.
   - You are entering the Super Chef Competition.
   - You are going to a new school.
   - You are campaigning to be class captain.
   - You would like to be chosen for a team.

> **Tip**
> Use positive, persuasive language to describe who you are, what you enjoy and why you would be the right person.

2 Brainstorm your **positive attributes** and make notes about what to say.
3 Use your notes to draft a paragraph promoting yourself.
4 Check and edit your work, then present it using neat, joined-up handwriting.

8 A promotional review

A You've learned how to promote yourself using persuasive language. Now let's look at how to promote a book!

1 Once a book is published, the publisher will usually promote the book. Can you explain why?
2 Read a review to promote the book on page 124. Then answer the questions.
   a What is the name of the book and who wrote it?
   b Describe the author of the book.
   c What made him write this book?
   d Is the reviewer positive or negative about it? Identify adjectives and adjectival phrases in the text that express this opinion.
   e Do you think you might enjoy this book? Explain your reasons.
3 Identify the key facts in this review. Summarise the review in just a few words to show the main points.
4 Read it aloud as if you were trying to promote it.

Session 8 A promotional review

COOK WITH JOSH IS THE WINNER OF THE 2013 GOURMAND WORLD COOKBOOK AWARD FOR BEST IN THE WORLD IN THE CHILDREN'S CATEGORY!

Cook with Josh is the brainchild of nine-year-old Josh Thirion. An enthusiastic cook with a passion for drawing, Josh compiled this unique cookbook of 48 recipes in the hope of inspiring other kids to **don** their chefs' hats and get into the kitchen.

Not only does *Cook with Josh* contain easy step-by-step recipes that all kids love to make, it also features lots of activities to keep the whole family entertained. Using his talent for drawing, Josh has created activities such as colouring-in, mazes, word games, crossword puzzles, spot-the-difference and connect-the-dots.

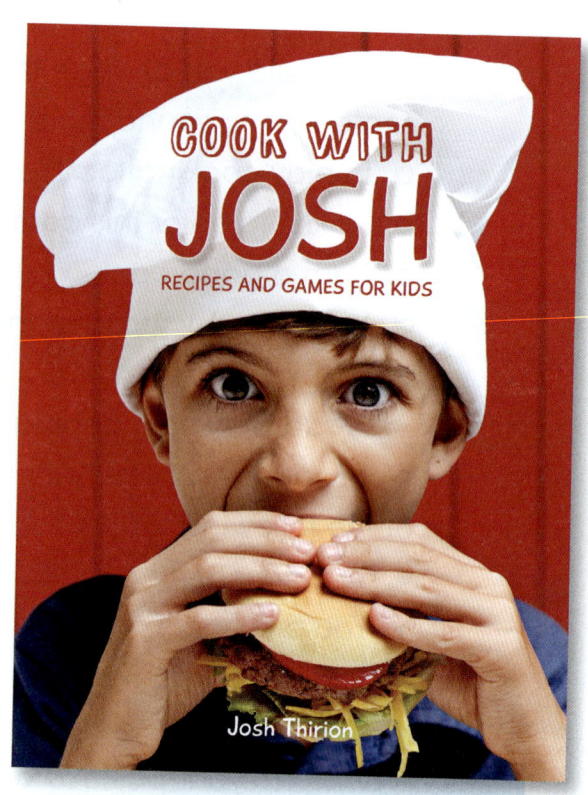

Deciding what to cook has never been this easy as Josh offers a **comprehensive** selection of delicious drinks, breezy breakfasts, **luscious** lunches, delightful dinners, divine desserts and tasty treats. Illustrated with mouth-watering food photography and Josh's own hand-drawn cartoons and step-by-step comic strips, *Cook with Josh* is a sure way to encourage a future generation of master chefs.

> **don** *v.* put on
> **comprehensive** *a.* detailed, leaving nothing out
> **luscious** *a.* delicious

Language focus

An adjectival phrase is a group of words acting as an adjective. Adjectival phrases act in the same way as adjectives – they describe and give extra information about the nouns.
An enthusiastic cook with a passion for drawing.
A cookbook of 48 recipes.

Unit 8 Food for thought

B 💬 Discuss other reviews. Find other examples of reviews or promotions. Use some of the questions in Activity A to analyse them in your groups.

C 📝 Record *Cook With Josh* in your reading log. Is this the sort of book you'd like to read more of?

9 Adverbs of degree

A 💬 Adverbs of degree add emphasis to the verb or adjective. Let's have a look at some.

1 Identify the adverb of degree in these sentences.
   a We saw an extremely funny show.
   b We had such a good time.
   c I am so excited to tell you about it.
   d It was definitely my best read ever!

*I am **very** hungry! I **urgently** need to catch a fish!*

2 Use a suitable adverb of degree to make these sentences sound more convincing.
   a She enjoyed the show.
   b It was entertaining.
   c We had a good meal.
   d I will go again.

B 👥 Have you enjoyed something recently? Tell others about it.

1 Choose a topic to review:
   • a meal you've loved
   • a party you enjoyed
   • your favourite game
   • a book you've recently completed
   • a movie or show that you went to.

2 Make notes to remember what to say. You can write down key words on speech cards.

3 Give a short review. **Persuade** your audience to try it out.

4 Just for fun, after your speech, take a vote to see who feels persuaded to try it out.

Tip
Remember to use some interesting adjectives and add some adverbs of degree.

Did you know?
You can find reviews for almost anything in newspapers, magazines and online!

10 Be persuasive

A Have you ever tried persuading your parents or teachers to change a rule?

1 With a partner, role play one of these situations. One of you can be the child and one can be the adult.
- Your weekly allowance <u>needs to be</u> doubled
- Homework <u>ought to be</u> abolished
- Vegetables <u>should be</u> optional, not compulsory
- Watching TV <u>could be</u> a school subject

2 List all the reasons that support what you believe.
3 Think of words that sound persuasive.
4 Role play the conversation!

Tip

To persuade people, you have to give them convincing reasons that will make them believe you and agree with you. To sound persuasive you can use words like the ones underlined in the sentences above: *must, ought, should, could, would, need*.

B Use connectives to make a point.

1 Identify the connective in the following sentences.
   a Eat carrots because they will make you healthy.
   b Apples are good for you therefore you should eat them often.
   c You will stay healthy if you eat lots of fresh vegetables.
   d Eat fresh fruit regularly since it is good for you.
   e Apples are delicious yet also very healthy for you.

Language focus

Some connectives are particularly useful when you want to make a point. They can add weight to what you are saying. Some useful ones are: *consequently, therefore, because, as a result, since, yet, so, although.*
You should eat apples **because** they are very good for you.

Unit 8 Food for thought

2 Link these sentences together with one of the connectives.

| although | therefore | if | since | because |

a Popcorn is a healthy snack. You can eat popcorn.
b Avoid fatty foods. Fatty foods are harmful.
c You need salt in your diet. You should avoid too much salt.
d Eat small amounts of sugar. Sugar is bad for you.
e You can have a healthy life. Follow a balanced diet.

Tip

Remember that when you link two sentences together, you remove the subject or replace it with a pronoun.

C Imagine persuading a group of young children to eat healthily. Write five sentences explaining why it is important. Each sentence must contain a connective from the above list, and sound persuasive.

11 and 12 Present a persuasive speech

A You'll need to use all the skills you have learned in this unit to plan and write a persuasive speech.

1 Choose a point of view. Use one of these topics, or think of your own.

SWEETS ARE BAD FOR YOU

SWEETS ARE PART OF A BALANCED DIET

SWEETS ARE **GOOD** FOR YOU

Sessions 11 and 12 Present a persuasive speech

2. Gather information. Do some independent research on the topic and ask other people for their views and ideas.
3. Plan your speech. Think about what you will say in each part of your speech.

Introduction:
State your point of view.

I should be allowed to have pink feathers.

Middle:
Give three convincing reasons why you believe it.

Firstly, it's colourful. Secondly, a change is good. Finally, it's important to express one's individuality!

Conclusion:
End your speech.

In conclusion, it's time to introduce more colour into the DUCK world.

4. Write a draft and get someone to read it and make suggestions.
5. Check your work and make corrections.

B Practise your speech.
1. Write key words onto speech cards as a reminder of what to say.
2. Practise saying your speech using your key words to guide you.

SPEAK CLEARLY AND USE EXPRESSION

Be enthusiastic and positive

Use persuasive language

Keep eye contact with your audience

Unit 8 Food for thought

C. A debate is a discussion where people express opposing views and the audience decides which 'argument' made the most sense.

1 Take turns to conduct a debate in front of the class.
   a Get into groups of three representing the same point of view.
   b Sit in groups facing the rest of the class.
   c Begin by taking a vote to see how many people in the class support each view at the start of the debate.
   d Each person from each team on the panel should take turns to present their prepared speech to the class.
   e Take a vote at the end to see if the audience's opinions have been changed.

Tip

Don't forget to listen to others and respond politely.

Sessions 11 and 12 Present a persuasive speech

9 Poems to ponder

Some poems are serious and others just plain silly. Some poems are designed to be read silently but others are more fun to read aloud in a pairs or in groups – a bit like performing a play.

In this unit you will read both silly and serious poems. You will practise a performance and write a sun poem.

Vocabulary to learn and use:
wordplay, poetic technique, simile, couplet, nonsense

1 Poems that play with words

A Poems aren't always serious. Sometimes they are designed to make us chuckle!

1 With a talk partner, read the title of the poem opposite and predict how this poem is meant to make us laugh.
2 Read the poem silently and then discuss each stanza.
   a What is 'wrong' in each stanza?
   b Which stanza is your favourite? Be ready to explain.
   c Rewrite your favourite stanza so that it makes sense.
   d Discuss how this changes the mood and effect of the poem.
3 Match each prefix to its meaning:
   pre   under
   sub   before
   non   against
   anti not
4 Choose at least one of the prefixes for each of these words:

   marine fix paid divide stop clockwise entity merge body

5 Make a word to describe the poem by adding a prefix to the word *sense*.
6 Select adjectives from the thesaurus to describe the poem.

   ridiculous, absurd, sensible, silly, ludicrous, mad, fun, serious, reasonable, laughable, idiotic

> **Any volunteers?**
> Who can use one of the words with a prefix in a sentence?

130 Unit 9 Poems to ponder

On the Thirty-Third of Januaugust

On the thirty-third of Januaugust,
right before October,
a strange thing didn't happen
that I always won't remember.

At eleven in the afternoon,
while making midnight **brunch**,
I poured a glass of sandwiches
and baked a plate of punch.

Then I climbed up on my head to see
the silver sky of green,
and danced around my feet because
I'd turned eleventeen.

A parade began to end
and music started not to play,
as rain came out and snowed all night
that warm and sunny day.

That was how it didn't happen
as I keenly don't remember,
on the thirty-third of Januaugust,
right before Octember.

Kenn Nesbitt

brunch *n.* combination of breakfast and lunch; usually served in late morning

Session 1 Poems that play with words

B Share your enjoyment of the poem with your classmates.
1 Join two other pairs and share what you like about the poem.
2 Practise reading the poem aloud as a group, and then perform it for another group.
3 Give each other feedback.
- Did they read the poem with expression and liveliness?
- Did they help you enjoy the poem's content?

C Do you enjoy this sort of poem? Record it in your reading log and add a comment.

Tip
Be creative when you perform the poem. Enjoy the madness!

2 Discuss poetic technique

A Explore how the poet created the nonsense effect by inventing words.
1 Identify the invented words.
   a Discuss how each word was created.
   b Suggest another invented word for each.
2 How can you tell each stanza is a complete sentence?
3 Scan the stanzas to identify the rhyming pattern and explain how the rhymes are important in the sound effect of the poem.
4 Read the extract below and compare it with the poem. What effect does the poem's layout have? Use the words *stanza*, *rhythm* and *rhyme* in your answer.

> At eleven in the afternoon, while making midnight brunch, I poured a glass of sandwiches and baked a plate of punch. Then I climbed up on my head to see the silver sky of green, and danced around my feet because I'd turned eleventeen.

Unit 9 Poems to ponder

5   Was the poem written to be read silently or aloud? Summarise your ideas in a short paragraph using evidence from the poem.

B Write another stanza for the poem.

Language focus

When poets use words to create a special effect, they are called **poetic techniques** or devices. They are like the *tools of the trade* for poets. They can include:

- sound effects: alliteration, rhythm and rhyme
- word arrangement: in lines, stanzas or shapes
- word meanings: words with several meanings or wordplay
- word images: figurative language and mind pictures.

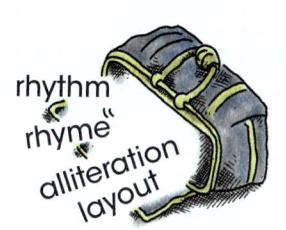

rhythm
rhyme
alliteration
layout

1   Work with a talk partner and plan a new stanza that could go somewhere before the final one.
    - Use at least one invented word.
    - Follow the same rhyming pattern.
    - Use the same sentence and line pattern.
2   Exchange your draft with another pair and give each other feedback on the ideas and the poetic techniques.
3   Finalise your stanza.
4   Read the poem aloud as a class, adding in all the new stanzas.

3 Prepare and perform a poem

A **AZ** Animals make great topics for poems, especially poems to perform. Work in groups.

1   Read *Rooster and Hens* on page 134 together, silently first to get the idea of the poem and then out loud to hear the 'effect'.
2   Check your understanding.
    a   Check the meaning of any word you do not understand.
    b   Choose a synonym for each of the words in bold.
    c   Describe what is happening in each stanza.
    d   Explain how the mood changes during the poem.

Tip
Don't forget your dictionary!

Session 3 Prepare and perform a poem   133

Rooster and Hens

The hens all rush around the yard,
They hurry hurry hurry.
They peck peck peck and cluck cluck cluck,
They scurry scurry scurry.
They fuss and **fret** and fret and fuss
With feathers in a **flurry**,
Until they rest upon their nest
And **cease** their senseless worry.

The hens each lay a single egg,
Then sit on it, contented.
The rooster treats this news as though
It were **unprecedented**.
With puffed up chest, he crows and crows
Till he appears **demented**.
He seems to think a chicken egg
Was something he invented.

Jack Prelutsky

3 Discuss the poetic techniques creating the mood in the first stanza:
  a the **repetition** of powerful verbs.
  b **alliteration** and **repeated** sounds.
  c the short, quick vowel sounds in the first part of the stanza.

4 Find where the mood changes in the poem.
  a Discuss how the poet uses the sounds of the words to help change the mood.
  b Choose words to describe the different moods in the poem.

B **Perform the poem with pizzazz!**

1 Work in groups and practise performing the poem. Experiment with different ways to perform it to bring out the different moods.
   a Include actions and sound effects.
   b Use group and single voices for different parts.
   c Highlight the poetic techniques and their effects.
2 Perform your poem for a younger audience and ask what they enjoyed about the performance.

Tip

You have performance licence! You don't have to say each verse only once – you can repeat the verses or parts of the verse as many times as you like.

4 Moon poem

Did you know?

Walter de la Mare wrote his poems over 60 years ago, but he wrote about timeless subjects so we still enjoy his poems today.

A Before listening to a classic moon poem, discuss what happens as night falls.

What happens to the light as the sun goes down?

How is moonlight different from sunlight?

What happens to all the colours?

How does the mood change from daytime?

Language focus

When adjectives describe how intense something is, we call it the 'degree of intensity'.

pitch black   black   dark   dusky   shady   shadowy   dim   dull   clear   bright

Session 4 Moon poem   135

1 Order these adjectives according to the light change from sunlight to moonlight.

shining burning glimmering glowing gleaming dazzling blazing

2 Listen to your teacher read the poem aloud.
   a Close your eyes and listen to the sounds and the rhythm.
   b Visualise the poem's images in your mind.

Silver

Slowly, silently, now the moon
Walks the night in her silver **shoon**;
This way, and that, she peers, and sees
Silver fruit upon silver trees;
One by one the **casements** catch
Her beams beneath the silvery thatch;
Couched in his kennel, like a log,
With paws of silver sleeps the dog;
From their shadowy **cote** the white breasts peep
Of doves in silver feathered sleep
A harvest mouse goes scampering by,
With silver claws, and silver eye;
And moveless fish in the water gleam,
By silver reeds in a silver stream.

Walter de la Mare

> **shoon** *n. pl.* old-fashioned word for shoes
> **casements** *n. pl.* a window that is fixed on one side and opens like a door
> **cote** *n.* a small shelter for doves or birds to live in

3 After listening, describe the mood the poem creates through its sound effects:
- the regular rhythm and flowing words sounds
- the repetition of *silver* and alliteration with the soft *s* sound.

4 Re-read the poem with a talk partner and choose a different adjective to replace *silver* each time it appears.

5 Read the poem with your new adjectives. How does the mood change?

5 Appreciate the poem

A Summarise your understanding in your notebook.
1 Write three or four sentences explaining the main idea of the poem.
2 Exchange your summary with a talk partner and compare your ideas.

B Focus on the images.
1 Use extracts from the poem in your answers.
   a The poem describes the moon as if it was a person. Find examples in the poem.

Any volunteers?
Who would like to read out their paragraph?

Language focus

Pronouns stand in for nouns to avoid repetition. Personal pronouns stand in for people, animals and things.

Subject personal pronouns	Object personal pronouns	Possessive pronouns
I, you, he, she, it, we, they	me, you, him, her, it, us, them	My, your, his, her, its, our, their

b Is the moon described as male or female? How can you tell?
c Do you like this way of describing the moon? Explain.
d How would you describe the moon?

Did you know?

A simile describes something *like* or *as* another thing.

She was *as* silent *as* a mouse. She whispered *like* the breeze.

Session 5 Appreciate the poem 137

2 a What simile does the poet use to describe the sleeping dog?
  b Invent a simile of your own to describe the sleeping dog.
  c Think of a simile to describe the harvest mouse or the fish in the stream.

3 Add **less** as a suffix to the following nouns:
  use air blame care colour fear price
  a Explain how adding **less** changes the meaning of the words.
  b What word with the suffix **less** describes a night with no moon?
  c Which word in the poem has the suffix **less**?
  - Explain the meaning of the word.
  - Think of a more usual synonym for this word.

> **Tip**
> Similes make poems interesting; they help us see things in a new way.

> **Tip**
> The poem has a strong rhythm. Try saying the first four lines again and find the rhythm – it's the same throughout the poem.

C Poems and songs share many features – poems often used to be sung not said.

1 In what way does this poem remind you of a song? Use the words *rhythm* and *images* in your answer.

2 This poem has seven pairs of rhyming **couplets**.
  a Explain how the rhymes add to the poem's effect.
  b Choose another word to rhyme with each couplet.

> **Did you know?**
> **Sonnet** comes from the Italian word *sonetto* which means 'little song'. This poem is not a true sonnet but it shares some sonnet features in that it has 14 lines and follows a rhyming pattern.

> **Tip**
> A **couplet** means two of something. What do you think a rhyming couplet is in a poem?

D Record the poems *Rooster and Hens* and *Silver* in your reading log book. Write a comment to say whether you enjoyed them and why.

Remember to use neat, joined-up writing in your reading log so that you can read what you have written easily when you look back at it. Others can then read it too.

Unit 9 Poems to ponder

6 Write a sun poem

A Follow *Silver* as a model for a poem about the sun.

> Will you describe the sun as a boy or a girl, or even an animal?

1 Draw up a plan.

Rhyming couplet 1 Idea:
sun shining brightly as it wakes up and says hello
Brightly, ~~radiantly~~ blazingly, here the sun greets the day now the night is done.

Rhyming couplet 2

Rhyming couplet 3

Rhyming couplet 4

Rhyming couplet 5

Rhyming couplet 6

Rhyming couplet 7

a Plan an image for each couplet. Describe the sun and what it does with its rays of light.

b Choose a rhyme for each couplet and brainstorm as many words as possible to ensure the best word choice.

c Describe the sun as a person or animal and include at least one simile.

d Use sound effects like repetition, alliteration and a regular rhythm.

Tip

It helps to go through the alphabet in your head! Sun: *bun, done, fun, pun, run, shun, stun, tonne, undone, won …*

2 Write your first draft and swap it with a talk partner.

a Read your partner's poem aloud to check for flow and rhythm.

b Underline any words that could be improved or corrected.

c Make at least two suggestions for improvements.

3 Revise your poem and read it aloud to the class or illustrate it imaginatively for display. Use presentation handwriting.

Term 1 Spelling activities

A Root words

Understanding root words will help you to form tenses.

The Latin verb **scribere** means 'to write'.

> **Tip**
> A root word is the basic form of a word. It can have prefixes or suffixes added to it to form other words.

1 Discuss how these words share the same Latin origin: describe, script, scribble, manuscript, prescription.
2 Use a dictionary to check each word's meaning and write a sentence for each.

Note: To form the past and present tense of verbs, -ed and -s are added to the root verb: look, look**s**, look**ed**. Sometimes, the root word has to change.

3 Use the example below to help you fill in the missing verbs correctly.
   cry: cried, cries
   a Sureshni always [try] her hardest.
   b Yesterday Faiek [reply] to my invitation.
   c Mariana always [carry] her dictionary in her pocket.
4 Discuss a rule for what happens to the y.
5 Use your rule to turn these adjectives into adverbs ending in the suffix **ly**.
   Easy, happy, lazy, lucky, clumsy, gloomy.

B Compound words

Two words can join together to form a new word.

> seaside, seaweed, seafood, seagull, seaworthy, seaman

1 Identify the root word and the prefix in each example.
2 Discuss how the prefix alters the meaning of each root word.

C Syllables

Words can be broken down into one or more small parts called syllables.
You can count the syllables "De/cem/ber." *3 syllables*

1 Write each month of the year and next to it the correct number of syllables.

Spelling activities Term 1

D. Letter patterns and sounds

Lots of words contain the letter pattern 'ea'.

Long **e** sound	Short **e** sound
clean	breakfast

1 Organise these words into two lists:

> treasure, clean, breakfast, beach, bread, please, seal, weather, stream, peach, instead

2 Brainstorm a list of other words with the <u>long **e** sound</u>.
   e.g. *week, meal, thief, receive, carry.*

3 Organise your words into lists under the different ways to make the long 'e' sound.

4 Which words do <u>not</u> belong with the long **e** words? Explain why not.

> steal, wheel, receive, please, cried, ferry, even, thief, breathe, feather

Tip
ea, ee, y, ie, ei are all ways to make the long e sound.

E. Silent letters

Some words contain silent letters, e.g. *wrong* and *right*

1 Choose words from the word bank to alliterate with these words:
   a Naughty   b Rapid

> know, kettle, wrap, knee, write, kite, wriggle, knot, wrestle, knight

2 Discuss why the words you chose could be used for alliteration in poetry.

Tip
Alliteration relies on sounds not spellings.

F. Word endings

Many nouns end with **er** (singer) or **or** (conductor)

1 Turn these verbs into nouns ending in **er**:
   a clean, speak, sleep, scream
   b teach, jump, work, walk, catch, tell
   c write, rule, bake, whine, weave
   d hop, skip, run, jog, slip

2 Discuss what spelling strategy you applied to each group of words.

3 Some nouns end in the suffix **or** rather than **er**. Use a dictionary to check which is the correct word ending for these words:

   acter – actor, mister – mistor, sailer – sailor, auther – author, docter – doctor

Spelling activities

Term 2 Spelling activities

A Adding suffixes

The suffix **-ful** can either form an adjective or a new noun.
Care + ful → careful (adjective)   Cup + ful → cupful (noun)

Tip
Remember to add **ful** not **full**.
My mouth is full is just a mouthful!

1. Turn each of these nouns into new nouns by adding **ful**:
   Spoon, glass, arm, hand, fork, ear
2. Most root words do not change before the suffix is added but describe what changes in these words: Plenty – plentiful; skill – skilful
3. Turn each of these words into adjectives by adding **ful**:
   Power, use, pity, cheer, beauty, will, hope
4. Choose two nouns and two adjectives ending in -ful and write a short paragraph including your chosen words.

Note: The suffix **-ly** is used to create adverbs from adjectives. The spelling of the root word does not change, with these exceptions: capable – capably   pretty – prettily

5. Discuss the rule being applied in each case.
6. Brainstorm some adjectives ending in **y** or **ble** and check if your rules work.
7. Use the words below to decide what rules to apply for these suffixes:
   ous, ness, less.
   Use these words to help you decide:
   (ous) nerve, ridicule, adventure, mystery,
   (ness) fussy, happy, early,   **(less)** pity, care, mercy, clue, life

B logy word families

Archaeology means the study of ancient cultures by looking for and examining their buildings, tools, and other objects. The suffix **logy** comes from ancient Greek and means the 'study of'.

1. Match each of these subjects of study to its name in the box:
   a music **b** Earth **c** handwriting **d** animals **e** myths and legends **f** living things.

   zoology, musicology, graphology, biology, mythology, geology

142 Spelling activities Term 2

2 Brainstorm or do your own research to find out about other subjects of study ending in **logy**. Use a dictionary to research the word origins.

Tip

If **bio** means *life* in ancient Greek, what do you think **bio**graphy means?

C AZ Build word families

You can build words from other words with a similar meaning: **biology** n. the study of living things; **biologist** n. a scientist who studies living things; **biological** adj. relating to the study of living things such as plants and animals.

1 Write the noun describing someone who studies each of the subjects in question 1 of Activity B opposite.
2 Write an adjective related to each of the nouns.

D AZ Vowel sounds

Knowing your vowel sounds can help with poetry. Many words share the same vowel sound but have different letter patterns.

1 Read these words aloud and group them into two lists in your notebook according to their vowel sounds. Underline the letter pattern making the sound.

> zoo, bowl, dew, stove, drew, roll, approve, stone, broom, rescue, soak, suit, hope, cove, stoat, blue, moat, bruise, coal, queue, toe, cloak, throne, crew, tooth, comb, argue, blow, cold, soon

2 Write a short poem using these vowel sounds, either for end rhymes or rhyming sounds within the lines.

E AZ Homophones can trip you up!

Some words sound the same but are spelled differently.

1 Underline the homophones in each sentence.
   a I am too weak to finish my homework this week.
   b An icy wind blew in the playground leaving us blue with cold.
   c I would help you bring in the wood if I had time.
   d I am too tired to do the last two sums on the page.
2 Choose the right word for each sentence.
   a Would you like a [*piece/peace*] of cake?
   b The children collected shells on the sea [*sure/shore*].
   c We are not [*allowed/aloud*] to talk in assembly.
   d We always [*groan/grown*] at our teacher's jokes.
   e Lauren kicked a ball accidentally through the window [*pain/pane*]

Tip

Use your dictionary if you are not sure [*which/witch*] one to use!

Term 3 Spelling activities

A Comparative spelling

Regular comparative and superlative adjectives add the suffixes **er** and **est** to the root adjective, e.g. *slow – slower – slowest*

Tip: Not **y** again!

1 Describe what happens when -er and -est are added to these adjectives:
   a *pretty – prettier – prettiest*   b *wise – wiser – wisest*
   c *thin – thinner – thinnest*   d *short – shorter – shortest.*
2 Explain the difference between the spelling change in c and d.
3 List these adjectives in alphabetical order in your notebook and write the correct comparative and superlative forms next to each.

> Juicy, large, cheap, strange, fat, dry, polite, grand, smelly, hot, sad, close, dirty, sunny, quick, sleepy, tall, great, cloudy, wide, wet, yellow, lazy, kind, fast, shiny, red

B Root words

1 Write these words into your notebook and underline the common stems.
2 Note down next to each whether it is a verb, a noun, an adjective or an adverb.
3 Use a dictionary to write down the meaning of any you do not know.
4 Choose five words and use each one in a sentence.

number: *numeral, numerate, numerical, numerable, numerous, innumerable, enumerate, numerator, numbered, unnumbered*

Tip: Phew! Number is a word with a looooong history!

C Nifty numbers

Knowing your numbers takes on a whole new meaning! Prefixes usually have a meaning which can help you understand the whole word, especially in maths.

1 Use the pictures to help you work out the meaning of the prefix.

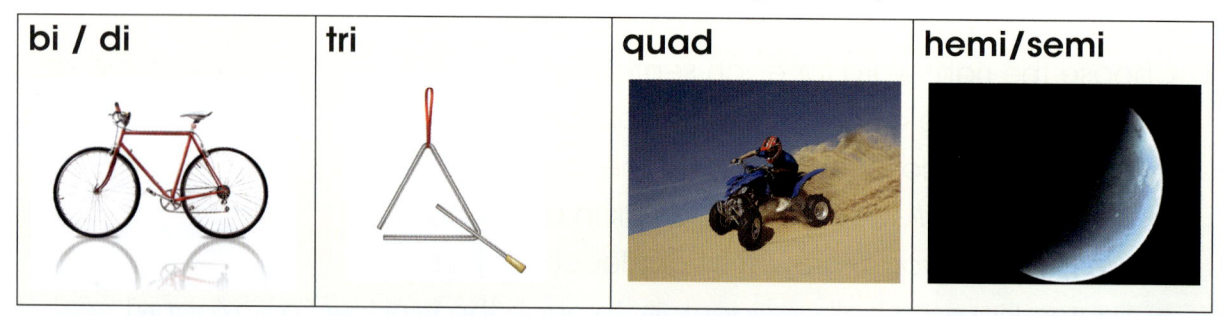

bi / di	tri	quad	hemi/semi

144 Spelling activities Term 3

2. Use sums to help you understand these prefixes: **milli cent kilo**
   1 metre ÷ 1000 = 1 millimetre   metre ÷ 100 = centimetre
   metre x 1000 = kilometre

3. Which of these words are not in the family of words with cent as the root?
   century, centigrade, centre, centipede, centenary, central, percentage, cent

4. Use a dictionary to look up these words and work out the meaning of the prefix **dec-:** *decade, decimal, decathlon, decagon, decimate*

D AZ Cardinal and ordinal numbers

Cardinal numbers are the numbers we use in calculations. **Ordinal numbers** give us information about order. Both can be written in numerals or words.

1, **2**, **3** or **one**, **two**, **three**

1st, **2nd**, **3rd** or **first**, **second**, **third**

1. Write down the numbers 1 to 10 in words.
2. Study the numbers below carefully.
   Twelve, thirteen, fourteen, fifteen, sixteen, seventeen, eighteen, nineteen
   Twenty, thirty, forty, fifty, sixty, seventy, eighty, ninety
   a. Identify the suffixes in both sets of numbers.
   b. Explain to a talk partner what you notice about the underlined root words.
   c. What do you notice about 14 & 40 and 18 & 80?
3. Except for **first**, **second**, and **third**, add the suffix **th** to form an ordinal number.
   a. Predict how 4th, 5th, and 8th will be spelled, then use a dictionary to check.
   b. Explain to a talk partner what happened in each case.
   c. Use your prior knowledge of spelling rules to predict what will happen to twen**ty**, thir**ty**, for**ty**, etc when the suffix **th** is added. Check if you were right.

Tip
Numbers written in words are usually hyphenated to show the numbers have been joined to form a new number: *twenty-two, forty-eight, seventy-three,* etc.

E AZ Short and long vowel sounds

Recognising spelling patterns for short and long vowel sounds is useful 'for rhyming and spelling better'!

1. Sort the words into two groups with the long and short **a** sound
   flat, player, apple, their, rain, eighty, explain, flake, grain, shape, trade, aim, lemonade, smash, weigh, strap, vein, away, cake, today, praise, stack
2. Identify four different ways of making the long **a** sound.

Spelling activities   145

Toolkit

Parts of speech and articles

Use these handy reminders to get on top of your grammar!

Nouns	Pronouns	Adjectives
Naming words for people, places and things: *duck flower hope Maria noise*	Stand in for nouns to stop repetition: *she he it they we*	Describe nouns to tell you more about them: *glistening cold gentle terrifying*
Conjunctions	**Prepositions**	**Adverbs**
Connectives that link words, groups of words or sentences: *and so however but although nevertheless*	A word or group of words used before a noun or pronoun to show place, direction, time, and so on: *before across over by through during beneath in*	Describe or give more information about a verb, adjective, phrase, or other adverb. Can act as a connective *slowly luckily merrily*
Verbs	**Definite article**	**Indefinite article**
Describe action or a state of being or having something: *wait repair skip breathe have be take shiver*	The word *the*. *That's a big name for a small word!*	The words *a* and *an*. *That's an even bigger name for some even smaller words!*

146 Toolkit

Punctuation

Full stops	**Capital letters**	**Commas**
Mark the end of sentences: I love eating ice cream**.**	Show the beginning of a sentence, proper nouns and titles: **M**y favourite cookery book is **D**reamy **I**ce **C**reamy by **R**afaela **V**ega.	Separate list items Show how to find meaning in a sentence: My cousin Leena**,** who often makes ice cream**,** puts in nuts**,** cherries**,** strawberries and raspberries.
Exclamation marks	**Question marks**	**Speech marks**
Indicate exclamations or commands: This ice cream is delicious**!** Give me some more**!**	Indicate questions: What kind of ice cream do you like**?**	Show words spoken in dialogue: **"**I like chocolate ice cream.**"**
Apostrophes Show possession Indicate contractions: Leena**'**s fruit **'**n**'** nut ice cream looks delicious! I**'**d like to try it.		

Toolkit 147

Reading skills

Do you know which reading skill to use and when?

What do you want to do?	This is the skill to use:	How to do it:
Get the gist of the text	skimming	• Look over the text quickly • Notice its features: headings pictures key words phrases
Find specific information	scanning	Run your eyes quickly along the lines looking for specific key words.
Understand unfamiliar words	reading in context	Read a few sentences before the word. Try to work out its meaning from how it is used. If it does not make sense as you read on, go back, re-read and change your idea.
Understand the whole text	close reading	Read everything carefully, concentrating on all the details.
Work out what's going to happen	prediction	Look for details in the title, blurb, text and illustrations that might be clues. What do the clues suggest? What could they mean?
Write or say the main points	summarising	Skim paragraphs for the main idea. Explain the main idea of each paragraph in a few words of your own.
Understand what you see	visual literacy	Details help show meaning: • Expressions and reactions • Movements & positions • How people or things are connected • Colours Labels, captions and other text
Use what you know to understand the text	using prior knowledge	What you already know can help you to: • understand a character's feelings • imagine a setting • understand why things happen • see how the information is useful • connect information in new ways Thinking about how your experience is different from the text can help you to understand it, too!

Don't forget reading for enjoyment! That's my favourite reading skill!

148   **Toolkit**

Poet's corner

Poets use words in special ways known as **poetic techniques**.

Words to describe poetic techniques

When we speak **literally**, we mean exactly what we say. When we speak **figuratively,** we use words imaginatively to create unusual images with different meanings.

It really helps to know your 'poem talk'!

simile someone or something is *like* or *as* something else
as cool as a cucumber
as brave as a lion   ran like the wind
glittered like the stars

metaphor comparing one thing to another without using *like* or *as*
The moon was a ghostly galleon.
The sun is a glowing furnace.

personification a metaphor where an object or thing is given human characteristics.
The stars smiled down at the sleeping earth. Winter's icy fingers stretched out across the fields.

idiom a phrase or group of words that together means something different from the meanings of the individual words.
Her eyes popped out of her head.
I'm glad you're on the ball today!

sound effects sounds that words make – often very important in poetry.

alliteration a consonant sound that is repeated at the beginning of several words for effect.
Hima hopped happily up the hill.
Jack jumped over the jungle gym.

onomatopoeia words that sound like their meaning.
The snake hissed, water glugged and leaves rustled.

rhyme words with the same or similar sounds at the end.

rhyme scheme the pattern created by the rhymes at the ends of words, usually described with letters to show the pattern, e.g. AABB.

rhythm a 'beat' or sound pattern made by stressed and unstressed syllables when we say the words.

syllable the unit of sound in words with one beat for each part of the word.

$\overset{1}{now}$ $\overset{1}{sil}/\overset{2}{ver}$ $\overset{1}{si}/\overset{2}{lent}/\overset{3}{ly}$

Toolkit 149

Looking for information

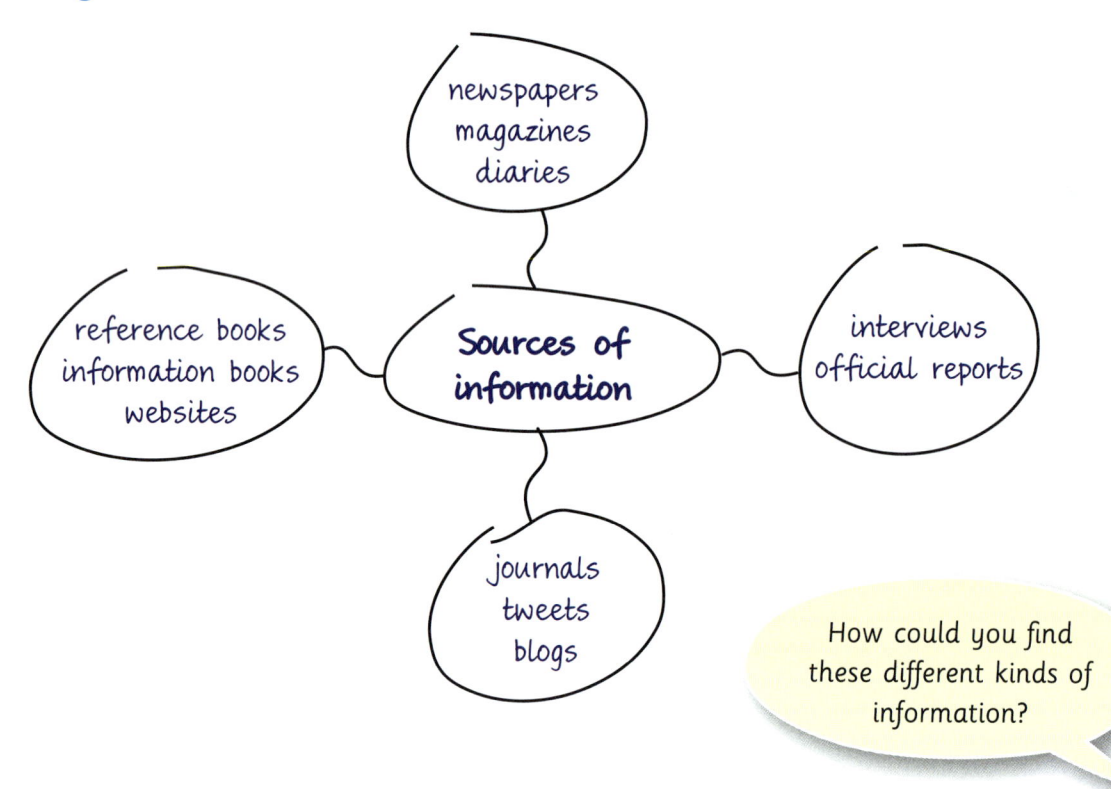

Sources of information:
- newspapers, magazines, diaries
- reference books, information books, websites
- interviews, official reports
- journals, tweets, blogs

- facts and figures
- details about a specific topic
- recent events
- historical events
- personal experiences
- people's experiences in the past
- people's opinions now
- word meanings

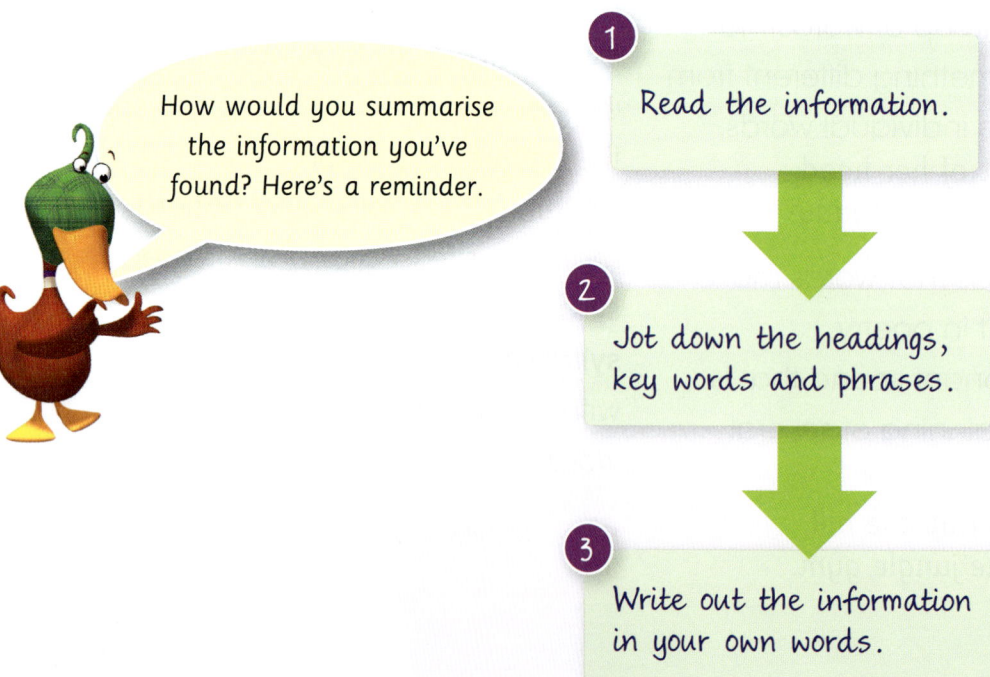

How could you find these different kinds of information?

How would you summarise the information you've found? Here's a reminder.

1. Read the information.
2. Jot down the headings, key words and phrases.
3. Write out the information in your own words.

Toolkit

The writing process

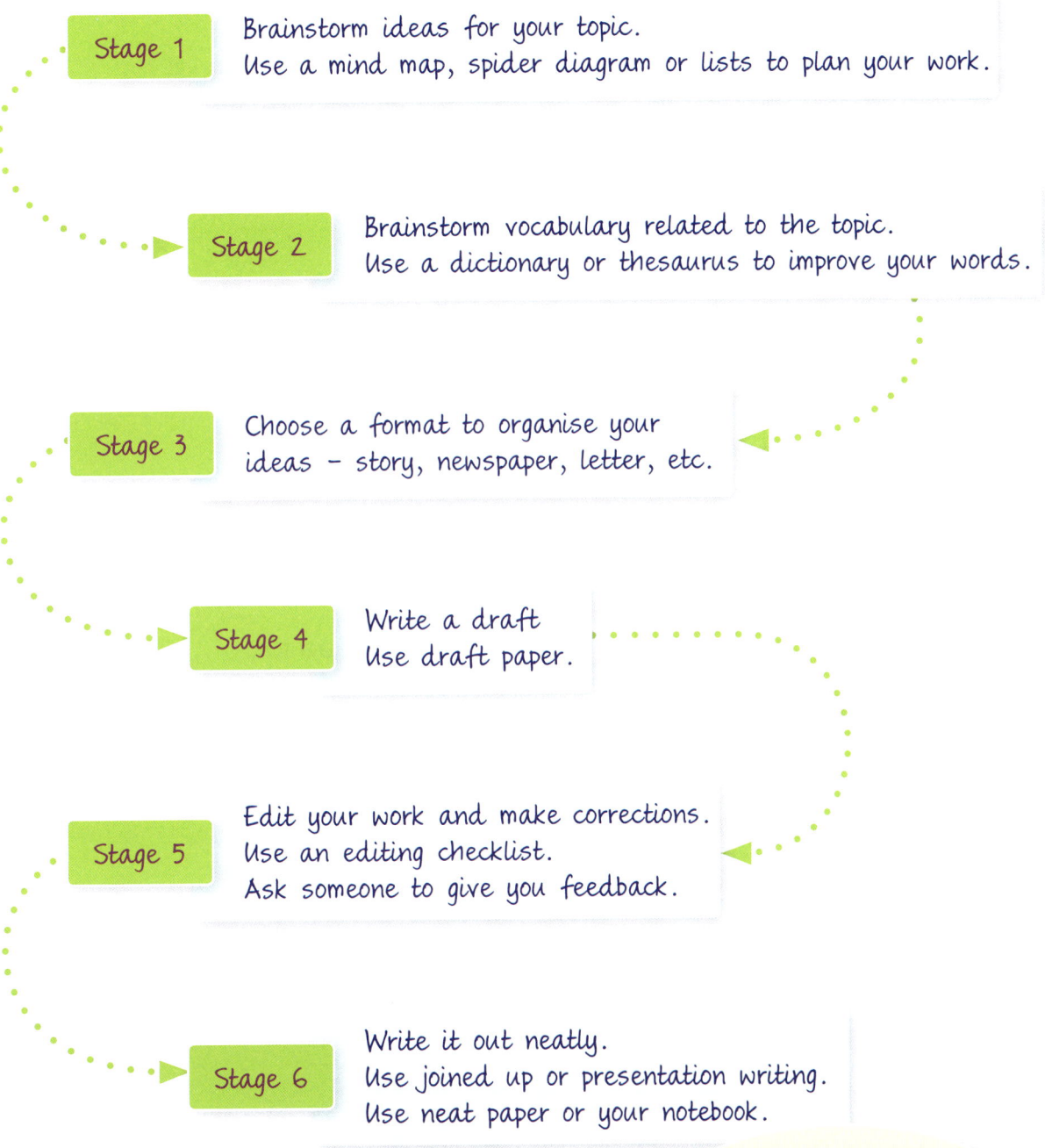

Stage 1 — Brainstorm ideas for your topic.
Use a mind map, spider diagram or lists to plan your work.

Stage 2 — Brainstorm vocabulary related to the topic.
Use a dictionary or thesaurus to improve your words.

Stage 3 — Choose a format to organise your ideas – story, newspaper, letter, etc.

Stage 4 — Write a draft
Use draft paper.

Stage 5 — Edit your work and make corrections.
Use an editing checklist.
Ask someone to give you feedback.

Stage 6 — Write it out neatly.
Use joined up or presentation writing.
Use neat paper or your notebook.

And when you've done all that, feel proud of what you've achieved!

Toolkit 151

Reading aloud essentials

Keep a steady pace – not too fast or slow.
Try not to stop and start.
Sound out unfamiliar words.
Use the punctuation marks for expression.
Check everyone can hear you.
Say the words clearly.

Hear ye! Hear ye! You need to work hard to listen well!

Exercise your listening skills

- Do you know what to listen out for?

- Have you got a notebook and pen ready?

- Are you sitting properly?

- Are you looking at the speaker?

- Don't talk to others while someone is speaking.

- Don't interrupt – put up your hand only if you really need to.

- Don't fiddle with things or distract others.

Editor's handbook

Use this useful handbook to check your own work or someone else's!

1. Have you done what you were asked to do?

2. Read through your work silently.
   - Are your spellings correct? Underline any you're not sure of and check them in a dictionary.
   - Have you used common words such as then, said, nice, and? Think of more interesting alternatives.
   - Which other words would you like to improve? Underline them and use a thesaurus to find more descriptive words.

3. Read your work aloud to check for sense and flow.
   - Do all your sentences make sense?
   - Are any words wrong?
   - Have any words been missed out?
   - Are any sentences too long to read easily?
   - Have you linked ideas and sentences using connectives?
   - Are you writing narrative or dialogue? Have you used the correct verb tenses?

4. Is your punctuation accurate?

5. Have you used capital letters for all the proper nouns?

6. Make all your changes and read through one last time.

Toolkit

Acknowledgements

The authors and publishers acknowledge the following sources of copyright material and are grateful for the permissions granted. While every effort has been made, it has not always been possible to identify the sources of all the material used, or to trace all copyright holders. If any omissions are brought to our notice, we will be happy to include the appropriate acknowledgements on reprinting.

p10 excerpt from *The Legend of Spud Murphy* by Eoin Colfer, (Puffin Books, 2004) reproduced by permission of Penguin Books Ltd, text copyright © Eoin Colfer, 2004, also published by Hyperion Book, an imprint of Disney Book Group, 2005. Copyright 2005 Hyperion Books, an imprint of Disney Book Group. All rights reserved. Reproduced by permission.

p16 excerpt from WHERE THE MOUNTAIN MEETS THE MOON by Grace Lin. Copyright © 2009 by Grace Lin. By permission of Little, Brown and Company. All rights reserved.

p45 'Mum' and 'Dad' taken from *Mad, Bad and Dangerously Haddock* by Andrew Fusek Peters, published by Lion Hudson 2006. Copyright © 2006 Andrew Fusek Peters. Used by permission of Lion Hudson plc.

p50 'What is Red?' from HAILSTONES AND HALIBUT BONES by Mary O'Neill, text copyright © 1961, renewed 1989 by Mary Le Duc O'Neill. Used by permission of Random House Children's Books, a division of Random House LLC. All rights reserved. Any third party use of this material, outside of this publication, is prohibited. Interested parties must apply directly to Random House LLC for permission. Also published by Egmont UK Ltd and used with permission.

p52 'Who knows?' by Fatou Ndiaye Sow, translated into English by Véronique Tadjo.

pp55, 59 from *Harry's Mad* by Dick King-Smith, by permission of A P Watt at United Agents on behalf of Fox Busters Ltd.

p65 from *The Voyages of Doctor Dolittle* by Hugh Lofting.

p73 Akhmim mummy material reproduced from a brochure by the Durban Natural Science Museum.

p85 headline and text from article 'Boy, nine survives wilderness thanks to tips from Bear Grylls' by Paul Thompson in the Daily Mail, June 2009 © Solo Syndication 2009.

p86 'Mangroves' by Zelda Quakerwoot.

p.87 'The Washing Machine' by Jeffrey Davies, from READ Magazine. Copyright © 1962 and renewed 1990 by Xerox Corporation. Reprinted by permission of Scholastic Inc.

p91 'Foul Shot' by Edwin Hoey from READ Magazine. Copyright © 1962 and renewed 1990 by Xerox Corporation. Reprinted by permission of Scholastic Inc.

p93 'Careful when you pour' by Paul Cookson, from *What Shape is a Poem?* published by Macmillan Children's Books, 2002, with permission from Paul Cookson.

p97 excerpt from *The Kite Fighters* by Linda Sue Park. Text copyright © 2000 by Linda Sue Park. Reprinted by permission of Clarion Books, an imprint of Houghton Mifflin Harcourt Publishing Company. All rights reserved. Reprinted by permission of Curtis Brown, Ltd.

p103 excerpt from *Toro! Toro!* by Michael Morpurgo, reproduced by permission of HarperCollins Publishers © 2002 Michael Morpurgo.

pp107, 109 from *Cool!* By Michael Morpurgo, reproduced by permission of HarperCollins Publishers © 2004 Michael Morpurgo, and with permission from David Higham Associates.

pp122, 124 *Cook with Josh* by Josh Thirion, published by Struik Lifestyle. © Random House Struik (Pty) Ltd.

p131 'On the Thirty-third of Januaugust' copyright © 2012 Kenn Nesbitt, from *The Armpit of Doom*, Purple Room Publishing. All rights reserved. Reprinted by permission of the author.

p134 'Rooster and Hens' from THE CARNIVAL OF THE ANIMALS by Jack Prelutsky, text © 2010 by Jack Prelutsky. Used by permission of Random House Children's Books, a division of Random House LLC. All rights reserved. Any third party use of this material, outside of this publication, is prohibited. Interested parties must apply directly to Random House LLC for permission.

p136 'Silver' by Walter de la Mare is used by permission of The Society of Authors.

Cover artwork: Bill Bolton

The publisher is grateful to the following expert reviewers: Samina Asif, Lois Hopkins, Mary Millet, Lynne Ransford.

Photographs

p24 *background*, © Brian Balster/iStock/Thinkstock, *l* © Anthony Pierce / Alamy, *r* © Mark Conlin / Alamy; p25 *l* © MP cz / Shutterstock.com, *r* © demarfa / iStockphoto/Thinkstock.com; p29 © XIANGYANG ZHANG / iStockphoto/Thinkstock.com; p31 © Vilainecrevette/Shutterstock; p33 ©© demarfa / iStockphoto/Thinkstock.com; pp35 and p38; © Stoyanova / iStockphoto/Thinkstock.com; pp36 and 39 © XIANGYANG ZHANG / iStockphoto/Thinkstock.com; p40 *l-r* © scubaluna / iStockphoto/Thinkstock.com, © Doug Perrine / Alamy, © Kristina Vackova / Shutterstock.com, © Vladimir Wrangel / Shutterstock.com; p41 © Stocktrek Images / Thinkstock.com; p71 © The Art Gallery Collection / Alamy; p73 © rysp / iStockphotos / Thinkstock; p74 © boggy22 / iStockphotos / Thinkstock; p80 © Kenneth Garrett / National Geographic / Getty Images; p82 © Dutch School / The Bridgeman Art Library / Getty Images; p83 *l* © Volker Kreinacke / iStockphotos / Thinkstock *r* © Lucyna Koch / Getty Images; p84 © Charley Gallay/NBC/NBCUPhotoBank via GettyImages; p96 *l-r* © Oleksiy Mark / iStockphotos / Thinkstock, © tubafirat / iStockphotos / Thinkstock, © sirzatkayan / iStockphotos / Thinkstock, © Oleksii Sagitov / iStockphotos / Thinkstock, © 3drenderings / iStockphotos / Thinkstock, © Sean Gladwell / iStockphotos / Thinkstock; p113 © Jupiterimages / Stockbyte / Thinkstock; p115 © sonnenklang-photo / Shutterstock.com; p117 © Alena Dvorakova / iStockphotos / Thinkstock; p124 Cook with Josh by Josh Thirion, published by Struik Lifestyle. © Random House Struik (Pty) Ltd; p136 *l* © azgek / iStockphotos / Thinkstock, *r* © Gregor Buir / iStockphotos / Thinkstock; p144 *l-r* © Kues / Shutterstock.com, © Jiripravda / Shutterstock.com, © bikeriderlondon / Shutterstock.com, © Elle Arden Images / Shutterstock.com; p152 © Gelpi JM / Shutterstock.com

Key: t = top, c = centre, b = bottom, l = left, r = right.